INVISIBLE FOE

Ronald Cove

Michael Terence
Publishing

First published in paperback by
Michael Terence Publishing in 2020
www.mtp.agency

Copyright © 2020 Ronald Cove

Ronald Cove has asserted the right to be identified as
the author of this work in accordance with the
Copyright, Designs and Patents Act 1988

ISBN 9781800940161

No part of this publication may be reproduced, stored in a
retrieval system, or transmitted, in any form or by any means,
electronic, mechanical, photocopying, recording or
otherwise, without the prior permission of the publisher

Cover images
Tithi Luadthong, Laschi Adrian

Cover design
Copyright © 2020 Michael Terence Publishing

Sadly, since writing this book my beloved wife passed away on Christmas Day 2019.

This book is dedicated to her.

No man could have had a better wife.

While writing this story, it occurred to me that most of us will accept that an army, that is not receiving adequate supplies when on the field of battle, could not be expected to win said battle. That being the case I think therefore it's fair to say, with all due respect to their bravery, our young spitfire and hurricane boys could not have engaged such a well-trained force as the Luftwaffe, and come out victorious in what is now known as The Battle of Britain, without some equally brave men risking their lives, making sure those fighting machines our pilots flew were regularly supplied with fuel, without which those aircraft would never have left the ground, let alone won the battle. Of course, those brave men I speak of were in the 1940s loosely referred to as, tanker drivers.

Here, I would like to take the liberty of bringing one of those brave men to the notice of the reader. To save embarrassment to his family, who I knew quite well, I will refer to this man as Mr B. Anyway, it appears one day while delivering fuel to an airfield in Kent, a German bomber began unloading bombs on said airfield, so Mr B. and a member of the American air force dived straight under the tanker, which was full of high octane fuel, for cover and each lit a cigarette to steady their nerves. Not very clever one would say, but when you are being bombed, how clever can you be?! Nevertheless, that's what happened. So many of those men did, in fact, lose their lives. Yet to date, I've yet to hear of one of them receiving a knighthood, or any other kind of recognition for their bravery come to that.

With this in mind, I've dedicated this book to all those long-forgotten tanker drivers.

- R. Cove

Authors Note

Although I have classified the following story as fiction, there is nevertheless a strong element of truth which runs throughout this narrative.

The reason I say this is because I myself was present on many occasions when these incidents, which I have described herein, occurred.

Please also note all names in this book are fictitious.

- *R. Cove.*

Contents

1: MAN ALONE 1
2: AWAY FROM DUNKIRK 4
3: HAPPY BIRTHDAY 6
4: THE JOURNEY BEGINS 9
5: THE START OF A CHASE 15
6: A VILLAGE CALLED HORNCHURCH 20
7: A QUICK VISIT TO FOLKESTONE 26
8: A WELL KEPT SECRET 34
9: STRIKE ONE 40
10: A VISIT TO LONDON 48
11: A MATCH TO BRIGHTEN THINGS UP 53
12: A FRUITFUL NIGHT 60
13: LATE AGAIN 65
14: GRANDMA SUSPECTS GAS 71
15: MURDERERS ROW 77
16: A NEVER ENDING ARGUMENT 84
17: A BREAKTHROUGH 90
18: SWINGING AT AIR AND JABBING AT SHADOWS ... 96
19: A CHANGE OF IDENTITY 104
20: MAN IN A BLUE SUIT 110
21: CARNAGE AT HEATHWAY 116

22: THE UNKNOWN SIDE TO PLUMPKIN 125
23: A BEARDED MAN OF DISTINCTION 133
24: WHERE DID HE GO? 138
25: A DISCOVERY 144
26: A ROOM GOES MISSING 150
27: A GUN AND A KISS GOODBYE 157
28: NEW LODGINGS 163
29: RETURN TO SCOTLAND YARD 169
30: A FAST TRIP TO WARLINGHAM 175
31: TOO LATE – AGAIN 182
32: A MERRY DANCE 188
33: A CHANGE OF LUCK 194
34: AUGER'S MISTAKE 199
35: HE JUST FADED AWAY 205
THE BLITZ 209

1:

MAN ALONE

A man clad in just khaki trousers, British army ammunition boots and jersey, stepped from behind a bush doing up the buttons of his fly, nodded to a group of passing bedraggled British tommies, smiled and remarked "That's better". The British soldiers were from an artillery battalion and were retreating to Dunkirk. The man was accepted by the group of tommies as just another tommy, who like themselves was retreating under the weight of the German onslaught. It was in fact a general retreat of the whole British and French armies to the Dunkirk beaches.

However, the man who stood about six feet, seemed delighted to meet up with a group of comrades, and made a point of explaining to any of his new found friends who wasn't too tired to listen, that his name was Dick Fletcher and how his battalion the 'Hampshire' regiment had pulled out leaving him behind. His fellow travellers had spent the last two days fighting an overwhelming losing battle against German armour, so could therefore show no interest in his predicament. They could not even be bothered to enquire about the fact he carried no rifle and did not display any visible signs of the Hampshire Regiment, he therefore silently joined the small group of men in a sombre march to the Dunkirk beach.

Some two days later on their arrival on the beach, Dick Fletcher bid his new found friends good-bye, telling them he would rest awhile, then search for his regiment. He had in fact already spotted the cabin cruiser he had been instructed to look out for, so now edging towards the water he slipped off his boots and prepared for a long swim.

It was sometime later. While splashing about in the water just off the Dunkirk beach, he was trying desperately to obtain some sort of handhold on the side of a medium sized motor launch, which was tossing about in the sea close by him. Dick Fletcher real name Paul Egbert, Hauptsturm Fuhrer (Captain) in Heinrich Himmler's elite SS, at that moment was acting directly under Himmler's orders.

Cpt: Paul Egbert, a survivor of the 1914-1918 war had distinguished himself in that 1st World War by performing several acts of daring on the battlefield. Noticeably among those deeds was in the first battle of the Somme in 1916, where at the tender age of 18 years, acting totally independently, the then Cpl: Paul Egbert had nonchalantly, while in the guise of a British officer posing as a certain Cpt: Brown, rode calmly into various allied gun emplacements on a white horse. Somehow convinced whoever was in charge, that he was from HQ and the Commanding officer was not too happy with that particular gun's performance. The CO had therefore suggested that he, Cpt: Brown provided them with an alternative target. It was of course a pre-selected target, that Cpl: Egbert had already selected, and was designed to save many German lives.

For this courageous show of bravery he had been decorated with the Iron Cross, 1st class, and was also given a field promotion from Cpl: Egbert to Lt: Egbert. All this was bestowed upon him by no less a personage than Field Marshall Paul von Hindenburg himself. A citation went with this promotion, which contained a brief description of Cpt: Egbert. It read as follows:- Cpt: Paul Egbert, a man of six feet in height, light blue eyes, thinning brown hair, an inch long duelling scar just under the right eye. No other visible distinguishing marks, a very brave man with an exceedingly sharp mind. A man of various talents. A brief statement followed pointing out that Lt: Egbert joined the SS in 1937, and was quickly promoted to captain (Haupt-Sturm Fuhrer. SS).

However Cpt: Egbert when thinking back, realised when he performed all those daring deeds back in that first war, he was a much younger and fitter man. Plus the fact back then for some unknown reason, he could never really take that war too seriously. Now unfortunately with some twenty years having slipped by, this war did not seem quite the same. For a start the Captain was convinced this Charlie Chaplin look alike man 'Adolph Hitler' really was mad, and did indeed want to rule the world.

2:

AWAY FROM DUNKIRK

Cpt: Egbert had been struggling in the water for about half an hour now, without much success. The cabin cruiser he was trying desperately to board kept rocking away from him each time a bomb exploded in the sea nearby. The effect of this caused the captain to give vent to certain feelings concerning that brilliant Luftwaffe fighter pilot of yesteryear, now Field Marshall Herman Goring, the present Commander in Chief of the Luftwaffe and minister for air, who had in 1918 with 22 kills to his name taken command of the famed von Richthofen Flying Circus.

At that particular moment however, the captain could not care less about Marshall Goring's past achievements. At this very moment in time he could only curse the man for sending out so many of these overly eager, brave Luftwaffe pilots, to bomb the beach and machine gun the poor sods such as himself, who were stranded in the water.

The aircraft Cpt: Egbert was screaming obscenities at, at that particular moment had just deposited several bombs along the beach and had then audaciously manoeuvred his dive - bomber down to sea level and very skilfully, while skimming the tops of the waves nonchalantly, treated the men in the sea to several bursts of hostile machine gun fire, after which he then deposited two more bombs in the water close by the captain. For this heroic deed, this annoying brave Luftwaffe pilot received more kind words like "You bastard" from an angry Captain with a shake of his fist. None of which made the slightest difference. However the last bomb that struck the water exploded with such magnitude that it somehow managed to lift the captain bodily out of his watery incarceration, throwing him head first into the side of the motor launch, which had eluded him for nearly an hour.

After a few slaps around the face and several sips of cold water, Cpt: Egbert regained consciousness. To his surprise he found himself propped up on many cushions and actually sitting inside the cabin of the elusive boat, which he at once realised was well under way moving away from Dunkirk heading towards the distant shores of England, at about 8-10 knots, he guessed.

It was however, when a man wearing wellington boots and a roll neck jersey, whom Cpt: Egbert judged to be the owner of this small craft, offered him a small flask of brandy at the same time explained that he, the Captain, should sit tight. "I'll be dropping the others off at a small jetty, but you stay put, you get off further along the coast," Mr Wellington boots told him. So now with his head clearing and with the small boat cutting a neat path towards the shores of England, Cpt: Egbert settled back and began to recall just how he had allowed himself to be coerced into this mad scheme in the first place. So as he sat back smoking and watched as the English coast drew nearer, his mind began to wander and the events of the last three days came flooding back.

It all began he remembered at the end of May 1940 when he had been summoned to the orderly room, where he had learned that Reichsfuhrer SS Heir Himmler had sent for him and that he, Cpt: Egbert, should report to the Reichfuhrer SS Himmler at 11am that morning.

3:

HAPPY BIRTHDAY

The dimwit of a bloody friend who presented me with a red, green and black regimental tie to wear on my birthday, had somehow neglected to have the bloody thing labelled as a fire hazard. I discovered this minor error when I leant forward to blow out my 44 candles that adorned my birthday cake. The bloody tie somehow sneaked out from behind the lapels of my coat, drifted forward and caressed the flames on the candles, which some other clown had made sure were well and truly alight, causing the bloody tie to immediately burst into flame. I naturally jumped back uttering a few chosen words.

It was however, Detective Inspector Dave Selby who stepped forward to save me from complete disaster. He pushed through all five of my well-wishers who were at that particular moment all taking a giant step away from me, while at the same time giving out with lots of 'oos and aahs', and would you believe one bright spark even informed me that my tie was on fire. Dave simply clapped his hands together with my burning tie between them, thus extinguishing the flame. When he opened his hands again I was left with a half singed tie knot, bright red face, a burnt blistered nose, and one eyebrow missing completely.

I looked at Selby and was about to give him my opinion of silk ties and lit candles, when he raised his hand, smiled and said "No, don't thank me now Bill, just buy me a beer later". I smiled back at him "Lucky for me Dave you can still move so fast" I offered by way of a thank you.

Having been friends for nigh on twenty-five years, I'm sure Dave knew and understood it was my way of saying thank you.

I had first met Dave Selby on the Somme battlefield back in 1916 when he was Sgt: Selby of the Rifle Brigade, (then attached to the 60th Rifles) in which I was serving as just plain Rifleman Billy Auger. It was in fact Sgt: Selby, who had guided me towards obtaining the rank of 1st battalion 60th Rifles sniper. It was also on that Somme battlefield we both stopped one. It happened as we began to retreat. Dave took one in the upper arm, while I graciously offered my leg for dear ol' fritz to practice on. Anyway we both ended up limping around the Whitechapel hospital wearing the obligatory 'blues'.

Dave Selby now Detective Inspector Selby had been a hard hitting very clever middleweight boxer in his day. He stood about 5' 10", strong powerful body, a mop of coal-black curly hair, with the face of a quick thinking hard-living man. On leaving the army we had stayed in touch. He had become a pro fighter and had pursued a reasonable successful career until his retirement in 1926, then after a short rest Dave had decided to join the police force, and now held the rank of Detective Inspector.

I on the other hand, on leaving the army had continued my not too brilliant boxing career. However, being a few inches shorter and somewhat lighter than Dave, I always stepped into the ring as a lightweight. Anyway, when I retired from my courageous fight career, I too became a police officer, and continued as I began by once again taking orders from Dave. By 1940 I'd reached the great rank of Detective Sergeant. Of course, nowadays I always refer to my boxing career as courageous, simply because if a man loses 11 fights in a row, and then has the audacity to sign for yet another fight, I reckon he's either very courageous or plain bloody stupid, and a detective Sgt: can't be stupid, can he?

However, at this point, Dave gestured towards my birthday cake "Look Bill, blow out them bloody candles and then we'll nip down to the Crown and Anchor for a pint" he suggested. The candles went out with one puff, then we were on our way.

It was a few days after my birthday in May 1940 that Dave informed me he was expecting us to be called in to see the 'Super' one day soon. "What for I wonder?" I enquired. "I wish I bloody knew me ol' mate" Dave responded. "Maybe he's decided to promote us," I remarked drily. "You'll be bleedin' lucky," Dave chuckled.

4:

THE JOURNEY BEGINS

Late May 1940, the German minister of the interior, Reichsfuhrer SS Heinrich Himmler, sat at his desk in the new Reich Chancellery building in Berlin. Elbows bent, resting on his desk, fingertips touching pyramid fashion in front of his face, as though in prayer. His eyes betrayed a mind which was in a dark faraway place. Nevertheless a slight tap on his door brought this small egotistic man quickly back to reality. "Come in" he commanded in a not too manly voice. The door swung open to reveal an SS Captain who stood smartly to attention, while at the same time offering a somewhat indifferent stiff arm Nazi salute. In return he received a bent arm offering with a mumbled 'Heil Hitler'. On entering the room and closing the door behind him, the Captain turned to face the one time chicken farmer, now SS Fuhrer Heinrich Himmler. "Cpt: Egbert Sir, I believe you sent for me" his unhurried words drifted across to his superior. Himmler was surprised by the man's overwhelming confidence, although he had read ample documents which proved beyond doubt just how brave and capable this man standing before him could be. In fact, only moments before the captains' arrival, Himmler had been going through one such document, which told of how some weeks before the Somme battle, the Captain disguised as a French officer, went striding out despite any personal danger and ordered a French battalion who were building up for a fresh counter attack at Verdun to pull back. Having done so, he then faded out of sight, and next appeared in July that year, at the battle of the Somme.

Himmler addressed the Captain "Please take a seat Haupt-sturm (Captain)" he indicated an empty chair. "Danke mein heir" came a slow reply. Once the two men were seated Himmler removed a small pair of pince-nez which he had somehow contrived to balance on the bridge of his nose. After carefully cleaning each lens in turn, he replaced them with a well practised expertise. There then followed a moment of silence as Himmler studied the Captain who now sat opposite him. He could see at once that the Captains' whole persona gave very little credence to a Germanic breeding. He was well aware that the man sitting opposite him could speak fluent English and French so therefore would create no suspicion when on the assignment the RSS Fuhrer had mapped out for him.

Breaking the silence Himmler said with conviction "Now Haupt-sturm, I shall come straight to the point" he then paused just long enough to retrieve a long white envelope from his desk draw. "First Haupt-sturm you must read this" he invited, handing the document to the now puzzled SS Captain. Captain Egbert stood and accepted the envelope with a frown. He then slipped a sheet of paper from the envelope, returned to his seat and read as follows:- On receipt of these orders the recipient will make himself available to be transported to a suitable area near the town of Dunkirk, there to ingratiate himself with the retreating allied armies. He will then endeavour to be transported with said armies across the channel where he will gain entry into the British Isles. There will of course be some danger involved in achieving the above, however it is hoped the recipient of this document will be capable of taking any necessary steps in order to overcome any difficulties that may arise. This document must be destroyed after the seal has been broken. Further verbal orders will be added by Reichsfuhrer SS Himmler. The Captain smiled, slipped the paper back inside the envelope and looked directly at Himmler, who had reverted to his old habitual manner of constantly pushing back his pince-nez glasses with his index finger of his right hand. He returned the Captains smile.

"Now Heir Haupt-sturm, what comments have you?" the SS leader solemnly enquired. "Well Reichsfuhrer it would seem I am to be dumped in amongst the British or French army and take my chances, and then hopefully somehow be rescued by the British, taken across the channel where I shall endeavour to avoid all further contact with their authorities. I will then act as an independent agent for the third Reich". The Captain then turned to Himmler with a questioning glance "is that right Reichsfuhrer?" he enquired. Himmler reacted with a slight nod of the head "Your diagnosis of the document is impeccable Heir Haupt-sturm" he informed the Captain while holding out his hand in order to retrieve the document from Cpt: Egbert "Thank you Haupt-sturm" he offered as the document changed hands. "Now it just remains for me to give you a few dos and don'ts when you arrive at the beach" Himmler said lightheartedly, he then indicated the Captain should return to his seat.

As the Captain made himself comfortable the SS leader took a firm hold of said document and very carefully placed a flaming match to one corner. When the envelope was engulfed in flame, he dropped the burning paper into a large tin which stood alongside his desk. The Captain sat back and watched in amusement as this little ritual unfolded, he realised it wasn't the first time nor was it likely to be the last time, that a state document would be confined to Heir Himmler's desk-side incinerator.

"Well Haupt-sturm, as for the dos and don'ts, there's only one thing for you to remember, and that is, just stay clear of the big ships which are rescuing the British troops, our brave Luftwaffe pilots will be making them their prime target" Himmler paused, studied the Captain enquiringly then continued "Now, once on the beach it is imperative that you find this motor launch". Once again Himmler stopped speaking and handed a colour photograph to the Captain "As you can see, what you will be looking for is an unusual motor launch which has a bright yellow circle painted on top of the cabin, which the Luftwaffe have been advised to avoid. This launch will be lying further out in deeper water, it has a two man crew and shall appear to be suffering engine trouble, however, once you are aboard it will immediately get under way and head for England". Having said this, Himmler once again pushed back his pince-nez from the tip of his nose. The Captain assumed this action to be a nervous affliction.

Himmler, after a short pause addressed the Captain once more "Yes Haupt-sturm I think you are the right man for this little escapade I have in mind" Himmler informed him. He then went on to explain how the allied armies were making a brave but futile stand at Dunkirk. "It is a foolhardy gesture, but nevertheless offers us the opportunity to slip one or two agents in amongst them"

While the little man with the big ego had been engaged in the aforesaid monologue, Cpt: Egbert although seemingly paying attention had in point of fact, been studying a large oil painting of Adolph Hitler which intrigued him somewhat. The Fuhrer had been portrayed posing in an aggressive stance, as though delivering one of his great pre-war speeches, but something about the painting which hung on the wall behind Himmler's desk, was not quite right. However just what, seemed to elude him for the moment. He therefore smiled inwardly, sought further comfort in his chair, and paid more attention to Himmler's screechy voice.

"Now Haupt-sturm, I want you to pay strict attention" Himmler started up again in a monotonous tone. "Once you reach the Dunkirk area, you will of course be in grave danger from both sides. Although ingratiating yourself with the British and French troops, you will in fact become one of them. Is that clearly understood?" Himmler asked in an exciting manner. "Clearly" came a joyous reply. "It is therefore of vital importance that you find and board the waiting cruiser as soon as you possibly can. Do not forget Haupt-sturm, you will be clad in British khaki, which will make you fair game for any Luftwaffe pilot, or any German foot soldier you may come across, so be warned" the SS leader paused once again, adjusted his pinc-nez.

Fixing the Captain with a long stare Himmler ploughed on "Now one more thing I will draw your attention to Haupt-sturm". Egbert responded with a raised eyebrow and lent forward as though being privy to a state secret. "You see Haupt-sturm, I have recently been perusing a few documents concerning yourself and it would seem that you function at a finer degree of excellence when not hampered by authority" the SS leader paused, gave the Captain a knowing smile, "Am I correct Haupt-sturm?" he enquired. "Well yes Reichsfuhrer, you see I do prefer to work alone if possible" Egbert confessed. "Right, now it would appear that in the past, many of our operatives have come under suspicion by frequently sending reports back to Germany" once again there was a pause then with a spread of his hands Himmler asked "Are we also agreed on that Heir Haupt-sturm?" "We most certainly are Reichs- fuhrer" Egbert answered with enthusiasm and was about to continue, however Himmler's raised hand called for silence, having achieved this he rattled on "Good, it is for that reason I have decided to relieve you of all responsibility concerning your whereabouts when in England. In other words Haupt-Sturm you will have carte blanch the moment you leave the Dunkirk beaches. You will not have to answer to anyone" Himmler then stood and shook hands with Egbert. "I wish you luck Haupt-sturm and a very successful war".

5:

THE START OF A CHASE

As it turned out Dave and I had to wait a full week before the 'Super' called us into his office. He indicated two chairs, "Please be seated Gentlemen" were his first words on that Monday morning. Just the sound of those few pleasant words coming from this giant of a man, who stood some six foot five inches, possessed two chins and proudly exhibited the belly of a pregnant woman whose time was almost up, should have put us on our guard immediately. The fact that he had said 'please' and 'gentlemen' seemed strange, because normally he would just leave us standing in front of his desk, then in all probability ask 'what the bloody hell we wanted' after he'd called us in, in the first bloody place.

Dave looked at me with a frown on his face, I retaliated with wide eyes and a shrug of my shoulders. "Right gentlemen now as we all know our army has just taken a terrible beating at Dunkirk and our navy is doing its damned best to bring home as many as possible," James Rickman the Superintendent began. Both Dave and I gave a sympathetic nod. Nevertheless at that point I suddenly realised that the dear old 'Super' had something special in mind for Dave and me. "However gentlemen" he continued "what concerns us is the amount of enemy agents that may well have slipped back across the channel with our lads, passing themselves off as British tommies. Then once on English soil, lose themselves in the crowd" he paused, studied Dave and myself for a moment then added with a wry smile "so to this end gentlemen, certain officers from the Metropolitan police are being transferred to the most vulnerable places in England". At this point he shuffled amongst some papers on his desk and finally came up with two separate envelopes, first he handed one to Dave, then the other to me. "And you two gents, I'm pleased to say have been seconded by the Essex police to join them at some godforsaken place called Hornchurch. These are your transfer papers" he gestured to the envelopes he'd just handed us. Then for good measure put in "Apparently a school called 'Suttons' which adjoins the airfield have already been complaining about broken fencing" Once again the 'Super' fell silent. After a moment or two, to give us a clue the briefing was over, he added "Be sure to close the door on your way out" then gave a little laugh which caused his jelly-like belly to wobble.

I made quite sure the 'Supers' door was closed tight behind me, in fact the aggression I used on closing it, he'd be bleedin' lucky to open it for at least another bloody week. Once outside I grabbed Dave's sleeve "'Ere Dave, I wonder what's wrong with the old boy, he don't seem to like us two a lot" I ventured. Dave gave me a lopsided grin "Blimey don't yer know? Fine bloody detective you are, yer say he don't like us, the man hates the bloody sight of us". "But why?" I began. Dave threw both arms in the air and growled back at me "Cos he was a bleedin' Major in the Cavalry, that's why" Dave took time out to enlighten me. "Oh yer mean he was one of those military jockeys who don't like us riflemen" I concluded. Dave smiled again "You've got it".

I believe it was DC Tony Willis who found us a map with Hornchurch clearly marked on it. It even showed a line where a fence divided the airfield from the school. Tony also explained to us that Hornchurch was on the district railway line, and it takes about an hour from London. So saying Tony disappeared. But of course before we could actually pack our bags and leave, another surprise awaited us in the form of the Assistant Chief Constable, Richard Allen, who everybody referred to as Dickie Doughnut. This time however we found ourselves speaking with someone, unlike the Superintendent, who spoke our language. To start with, he was a more likeable man, stood about five foot seven inches, so for once I didn't have to stand on a chair to make eye contact, and there was no bullshit about this man.

On entering his office, after a firm handshake we were designated a chair each, and also told 'smoke if you like'. He next asked if tea or coffee was our choice. Tea was the choice, and when it arrived, Dave and I both took and lit a Goldflake cigarette that Assistant Chief Allen had offered. So now with three men smoking, within minutes the room was a smoke pit. Nonetheless at this point the ACC gave us a clue as to why he had acquired the nickname 'Dickie Doughnut'. it was only a small clue really, which amounted to six doughnuts that had been brought in with our teas and placed purposely on the ACC's desk alongside his tea within easy reach of his hand. Although Dave and I glanced at each other, no words were exchanged as Dickie munched on a doughnut, puffed on a cigarette, then happily sipped his tea, his light blue eyes studying us. Two doughnuts later after wiping his mouth with a paper napkin, this likeable man dressed in a dark blue suit, leant across his desk and began to explain why it was Hornchurch that needed the assistance of a Detective Inspector and a Detective Sergeant. "It does seem a long way out to send us Sir, when there's so much crime going on here in London" Dave put forward. "Well that's as maybe Dave, but you see, the people you and the Sergeant will be hunting for are not the common home grown variety of criminals". At this point the chiefs cigarettes came round again, and although we could hardly see each other through the thickening smoke, old Dickie bravely continued "No Inspector, you and Auger will have to use all your skills and a lot of patience to weedle out some very intelligent highly trained operatives, whom our intelligence people think have been shipped across with our boys from Dunkirk and are now operating in the Essex area". And there ended Dickie Doughnuts sermon. Dave and I then stood, shook hands with Assistant Chief Allen and made for the door. Just before we left however, he made a gesture towards DC Tony Willis who was at that moment heading towards us, while at the same time shuffling a bunch of papers about in his hands. "DC Willis has all the relevant papers that are needed" were the last words we heard from ACC Allen before I closed the door.

Now with all the essential documents safely confined to Detective Dave Selby's briefcase, DC Willis once again referred us back to the rail map "Here you are Inspector" he began addressing Dave "Like I said Hornchurch is on the district line" he marked the map with a pencil "Mr: Allen did try to arrange a car but no dice I'm afraid" DC Willis informed us with a shake of the head, then quickly added "Never mind I've got a couple of police railway passes here". He handed Dave a long brown envelope "Ah, thanks" Dave replied. As he handed me mine I chimed in with "Where the bleedin' 'ell do we catch this bleedin' train anyway?" Dave looked at me with a puzzled frown. So just to confuse the issue a touch more I added "And where for Christ sake do we get off?" Dave immediately turned to Willis and was about to speak when the DC raised his hand "Don't worry I'm coming with you, so you'll be alright" he kindly informed us.

"Nevertheless" he continued "our best bet will be to catch the underground train at either Westminster or Charing Cross, you pick" he invited. "Or failing that we could either jump on a train at Whitechapel or if you like Bow Road Sergeant" he said nodding in my direction. "Ok, I think we get the idea now Constable" Dave threw at him in order to curtail any other snippets of information that Willis might want to share with us.

6:

A VILLAGE CALLED HORNCHURCH

When Dave and I arrived at the Hornchurch Police Station, we found it to be an old wooden shack which had been thrown up just after the First World War. The structure itself lay back off the road behind a six foot fence. The first obstacle was a swinging gate. Having once negotiated the gate, step too far to your left, and in these bloody night time black outs, you could quite easily bang your head on a pole, lucky for us it was a bright sunny morning. The pole stood around twenty two feet in height, with the air raid siren perched on top, which happened to be sounding the 'all clear' as we approached. No doubt half the Hornchurch and Elm Park population would be vacating their Anderson air raid shelter about now. The time was nigh on 8am and in spite of a long continuous blast of the siren sounding 'all clear', we first heard then clearly saw a number of spitfires creating a tapestry, as they raced across a blue sky heading towards that well known Hornchurch aerodrome.

"That's a bleedin' lovely sight Dave," I remarked as we pushed through the swing gate. "Yes, it would be if that poor sod wasn't amongst them" Dave retorted shielding his eyes with one hand while pointing with his other hand to one spitfire that was being followed by a long trail of black smoke. "Sweet Jesus" I croaked "'Ope the poor bugger makes it". That's when we heard a voice from inside the police station "I think he'll be alright Sergeant, we phoned the airfield, told them he was coming" the voice of DC Willis informed us by sticking his head out of an open window. The DC had travelled down from London with us but had left the train at Elm Park, a station before Hornchurch, in order to procure a police car from some sort of car depot or car pool, I didn't know exactly which, the Essex police apparently had this facility at Elm Park.

Anyway after first meeting the police Superintendent of Romford, who had decided to travel into Hornchurch especially to meet us, we were then informed by DC Willis, that he had secured a car for us, but for some reason or other we must wait until the next day before it could be delivered. However, in the meantime Superintendent John Jarvis left us plenty to think about. For a kick off, he told me and Dave we must be constantly on our guard, because the top brass reckoned that jerry had by now already unloaded something like five hundred clever bloody agents on British soil by way of Dunkirk, and MI5 hadn't got a sodden clue where to start searching for them. "No my friends we'll only know where they are when they become bleeding active". This then was the delightful piece of information old Johnny Jarvis served up to us before he returned to Romford.

Once again Dave and I found ourselves relying on DC Willis, this time however his task was to find us somewhere to live while we stayed in Hornchurch, and again the young DC came up trumps. He'd not only managed to book us into a two bedroom flat on a six months lease, but the cheeky bugger also arranged with the Romford Superintendent Johnny Jarvis for the Essex police to foot the bill. It turned out to be a large house that had been converted into flats and stood opposite a beautiful park called 'Harrow Lodge', and in spite of the widespread bombing that seemed to be affecting even this small village tucked way out in the Essex countryside, we could see some teenagers happily playing cricket on one of the parks big fields.

We also found out later that DC Willis had acquired a room for himself a couple of doors away from our flat. It also appeared that this bright lad Willis had found himself a lady admirer in the form of Mrs: Daisy Drake, his young landlady, whose husband coincidently happened to have been lost at Dunkirk. Dave and I went along to meet said young landlady and offered our commiserations. In doing so it became abundantly clear to both of us that this Hornchurch lady had firmly set her sights on DC Willis and was relying on his broad shoulders for protection.

Back at the Hornchurch police station we received the news that an old boy named Daniel Ross may have seen a saboteur. Anyway dear old Daniel had said he saw some bloke taking photos of the airfield. So Dave and I were handed the unenviable task of ferreting out the old boy. We were given an address, 22a, Stanley Road, as it happened, it turned out to be a road just before the bloody police station in fact we must have walked by this sodden street on our way from the railway station that morning. "Never mind we've found it now" Dave sighed pointing to number 22a, and at that moment Dave stopped to light a fresh cigarette, while I pushed on through the gate. As I did so some snotty nose little urchin playing in the street with others, yelled out "Oi mister, they've just put a new spring on that old bleedin' gate". I stopped. Trying to comprehend what the kid had said, and of course by then the bloody spring had proved its worth, the gate swung back with such bloody force, it felt like a rocket had hit me up the arse. The gate propelled me up the path leaving me in a heap on number 22a's doorstep. The little urchin looked over the gate at me, wiped the back of his hand across his snotty nose and said "There, told yer mister, didn't I." Then him and his mates ran off laughing. "You alright Bill?" Dave spat out between fits of laughter. "Yeah, course I'm alright, I always do this sort of thing, gives them snotty nose little buggers something to laugh at" I offered back as I picked myself up, anyway I don't think Dave heard me, the silly sod was too busy laughing at my misfortune.

Mr Daniel Ross invited us into his living room, at the same time offering us a tea. He was a man of medium build, dark hair with a sharp serious face. We refused the tea but accepted a cigarette each, then dear old Daniel started in on his story. First we learnt he was fifty-one years of age, served as a company runner in 1914/18 and now lived alone, his wife having run off with a younger man two years ago. So nothing new to write home about there.

At this point Dave brought Daniel back to what we were there for and persuaded him into telling us about his encounter with this bloke he saw taking photos of the Hornchurch airfield. Old Dan looked from one to the other of us with raised eyebrows "But I've already told your Sergeant at the police station" he said slightly bemused. "Yes, we do appreciate that Mr: Ross, however I'm afraid we were only told that someone had seen somebody else taking photos of the airfield, they gave no descriptions or further details, so you see Mr: Ross we would like to hear it straight from you" Dave informed him, then quickly added "Look Mr: Ross, perhaps you would like to give Sgt: Auger here a statement" Dave encouraged as he moved a chair nearer the table so I could sit next to old Dan. The poor old sod shrugged his shoulders, lit another cigarette then made himself ready to deliver his story once again while I lay my notebook and pen on the table, lit a cigarette and nodded to poor Dan to begin his narration. "Well what happened" he began "I was out walking, must have been Wednesday or Thursday of last week. I nipped into Fred's café". I stopped old Dan there "Oops, 'ang on, you've lost me there mate, this Fred's café, where exactly is that?" I asked. "Oh yes, of course" he apologised. "Right, that's ok, now if we could just continue mate" I smiled, coaxing him into moving on with his story. He went on "Right, Fred's café, it's quite easy to see really, it's right opposite the railway station, you can't miss it, his name is clearly displayed out front" Dan explained before continuing his story. "Now where was I? oh yes, that's right, it was as I came out of Fred's café I first saw him. He walked across the road and started talking to a couple of school boys that were obviously on their way to school, he then walked along with them. At first I thought he was one of the lads Father, coz he kept indicating like he wanted to take their photo. You see he had this concertina camera that he kept lining up on them, which I thought to be rather strange anyway". Dan suddenly stood up "You blokes fancy a cuppa yet?" he asked making his way through to the kitchen, although before we could answer he'd called back "Good, I'm bloody gasping meself"

Having served up the tea Dan went back to his narration "Yes you see, this bloke followed these young boys right into the boys Suttons Senior School grounds" Dan went on smoothly. "'Ang about," I said "'Ow d'yer know that Mr: Ross?" "Oh, that's bloody easy, I followed them" he replied. "Good, now please go on" I requested. He did so, "Well it's like I said, the kids went on into the school and this old codger with the camera took a sneaky look over the school fence into the airfield, then before you know it this bugger had found something to stand on and is hanging over the bloody fence taking pictures, and that's about it" he concluded. I smiled at him, put a nice full stop on my paper and looked at Inspector Dave Selby. "Anything else Sir?" I asked. Dave shook his head at me, then turned to Mr: Ross "Just one thing more would be appreciated Mr: Ross, if you could give us an idea as to what this man looked like, you know, how tall and so on" was Dave's last request. "Oh yes I see" old Dan commenced "Well at one point I did stroll quite close to him, and in consequence can tell you that this man stood about six foot, had light brown hair, but apart from that, what intrigued me most was his camera, it had a pull-out lens and I'm sure it was a German Liecer camera, mind you it seemed pretty new, so there you are. I think, that's about it, I believe" he stopped, then quickly started again "no wait a minute, he had a scar on his face under one eye, I think". "Which eye?" Dave quickly asked slightly agitated. Dan waited a moment, visualising in his minds' eye I guessed, just where he had stood in relation to our phantom photographer. "That's it, it must be his right eye" he finally worked out. "Well that's good Mr: Ross now is there anything else you can think of before we leave?" Dave finished. "No, I don't think so" dear old Dan let us know. "Ok in that case, thank you for the tea and so much valuable information Mr: Ross, if you do happen to think of anything further, just ask for Detective Inspector Selby or Detective Sgt: Auger at the police station" Dave informed him. We then shook hands with Danny boy and left.

7:

A QUICK VISIT TO FOLKESTONE

It was someone shaking his shoulder that awoke Cpt: Paul Egbert, and strangely enough the captain was alert in an instant. "You're alright Captain it's only me" a voice close by softly whispered. "Ah right, must have dozed off" the captain confessed sitting up straight, glanced through one of the boats small windows, where he at once discovered the little craft had come to rest on the beach alongside a jetty. "Don't tell me we've arrived already!" he exclaimed. On standing he realised it was the man who had originally been wearing the roll neck jersey and wellington boots that was addressing him. "So what happens now?" Captain Egbert asked of this man, who was now dressed in a blue suit, spotless white shirt and grey tie which put a pair of highly polished brown leather shoes to the test. "Well there is a bundle of civilian clothes under that bunk you're sitting on Haupt-sturm Fuhrer, you'll also find some papers in a coat pocket with further instructions, may help later, and I don't know about you Haupt-sturm, but for me it's a case of returning to my regiment as quickly as possible" came an unexpected reply. "Yes well where exactly do I go?" the captain ventured. "Oh that's easy Heir Haupt-sturm, you go straight up the beach there, and make your way along Beach Walk, which is just over to your right" the man pointed. "Halfway up that slope you'll find the Folkestone police station, all you have to do is tell them you've escaped from Dunkirk, show them this boat if you have to. I don't think they'll question you further" he concluded.

"That's all very well, but they're not stupid" the captain replied. "No, they're not, I agree Haupt-sturm Fuhrer, but they are English, and knowing that their army is being slaughtered at Dunkirk, these arrogant Englishmen will take one look at you and automatically assume you are one of their brave boys determined to get back home and prepare to go back into action and deny the terrible Hun the pleasure of landing on British soil" he explained.

The captain had no idea just what this man had in mind nevertheless he could see the sense in what this man was saying. "Ok, so now we must part" he offered his hand adding "Mister" he then waited for the man to reveal his name. Although receiving a firm handshake, was surprised at what the man said next. "Sorry heir Haupt-sturm but as they say in England 'nice to have known you old boy but no names, no pack drill', and if I don't see you again good luck and remember, I was never here. You and a few other lads commandeered this boat at Dunkirk. You all agreed by making your way in this small craft across the channel, you all stood a better chance. Is that clear Heir Haupt-sturm?" The captain nodded with a smile. "Once again, good luck". Having by now jumped off the boat, the man looked up at Egbert and informed him he should make haste as the tide was now coming in. With that his comrade was gone.

Cpt: Egbert on observing the tide now creeping up the shore decided it was also time for him to vacate this small craft. He dragged out and quickly checked the bundle of civilian clothes from under the bunk, then having satisfied himself that he carried no form of identification, picked up a spare tin hat, commandeered a 303 rifle that some good Samaritan had considerately left behind. He leapt off this small motor launch, and immediately became aware and slightly bemused when a crowd started gathering and suddenly began cheering, with lots of hand clapping thrown in. There then followed several pats on the back with shouts of 'well done tommy' added. The captain thought how ironic and could not stop a broad smile caressing his face. He accepted their praise by thanking one here and there and shaking hands with others.

Quite suddenly with all his well-wishers left behind on the beach, the captain found himself lumbering up Beach Walk. On reaching Folkestone police station his mind already made up, and having recalled Heinrich Himmler's words, which clearly stated 'once in England Cpt: Egbert you have carte blanche', he therefore decided to bypass the police station, instead find a railway station. Nevertheless his immediate worry he thought, would be to sort out a place of lodging, preferably somewhere in Kent.

However, at this point he realised navigating his way past the police station would present some difficulty in itself. Conscious of the fact, that at any moment, a police officer could step outside the station and ask one or two awkward questions of him. Cpt: Egbert now using his nom de plume, Dick Fletcher, slung his rifle into the natural trail position of a rifleman, and with the bundle of civvies tucked under one arm straightened his back and marched with purpose straight past the Folkestone police station. It wasn't until he was several paces beyond said station that he breathed a sigh of relief. "Good, now for the nearest railway station" he mumbled to himself while striding into the Folkestone High Street.

On finding the railway station Dick Fletcher sought and found the men's toilet, once inside said toilet he quickly changed his clothes, then sat and read through the documents he'd been lumbered with, nevertheless a wallet in the inside jacket pocket crammed with English banknotes pleased him, but he was surprised to find that an application had already been lodged on his behalf to join the RAF. The document also informed him a sympathiser would contact him in due course, and interestingly it even supplied him with the name 'Big Harry' a café on the High Street, where he should order one slice of toast, a mug of tea no sugar or milk at lunchtime any day.

∗

It was about this time a Wolseley saloon car drew up outside the Folkestone police station. "This looks a cosy place Dave," I told my superior DI Dave Selby as we both climbed the few steps which led into the station. Once inside we could see it was a far more substantial building than the one we'd left behind at Hornchurch. However, apart from three or four police officers sitting around drinking tea and smoking, the only other thing that caught our eye was a large photo of Winston Churchill hanging on the inside of the room door, which some bright spark had deemed to be a good idea in order to hide a dartboard. Anyway it was a uniformed Sergeant who'd crept up behind us, tapped Dave lightly on the shoulder and enquired "Can I help you gents?" Dave spun round to face him. "Oh yes Sergeant," he said, at the same time holding out his credentials and telling the Sergeant who we were. "Oh I see Sir, well I'm Sgt: Nichols and I believe what you must have done is inadvertently walked in through the wrong door, therefore you and your Sergeant must have walked past the entrance desk without me seeing you Sir" the Sergeant rattled off. "Ah well, never mind Sergeant, no harm done," Dave offered up in our defence, his eyes searching round the room for the correct door we should have come through. Finally gave up, turned back to the Sergeant "anyway what we want is to see whoever is in charge here Sergeant" Dave told him. "Ah well, I'm sorry there Sir, but both the Super and our chief of detectives have gone to a briefing over in Margate, can't say when they'll be back Sir" the Sergeant informed us. Dave studied the man for a moment, then turned to me. "What d'yer reckon Bill?" he enquired of me. I thought for a moment then nodded towards Sgt: Nichols "Perhaps the Sergeant will know" I suggested. Dave looked doubtful, turned back to the Sergeant "Right ok then, in that case, maybe you can help Sergeant" Dave told him now looking very serious. "I'll do my best Sir" the Sergeant sighed, now seemingly getting cheesed off with it all. "Right, well look Sergeant, at Dover and other ports along the way, there seems to be a great number of our troops being ferried ashore from the big ships" Dave began rattling on, so I butted in and said in a subordinate manner "Excuse me Sir, but I think it might be better if you get straight to the point". Dave gave me a sly smile "You're right Sgt: Auger," he acknowledged, and to Sgt: Nichols said "Look Sergeant what we're looking for is any small boat that may have slipped across the channel alone, with let's say just half a dozen odd bods aboard, who could have come ashore unnoticed. Now can you help us there Sergeant?" Selby concluded. Sergeant Nichols looked at Selby and myself as though we were both completely nuts. "Can I help you, you say?" he began "Well I say I can Sir, you see the poor sods have been coming off the beach since yesterday afternoon, in fact this morning alone, bloody hundreds must have walked by this very station Sir" he shook his head "bloody pitiful sight it is Sir, to see a beaten soldier, why most of the poor little buggers can't even bear to look you in the eye" the Sergeant broke off there. We could see his feelings were getting the better of him now. "Oi Harry" he suddenly called "see if you can rustle up a nice cuppa for us three". "Right Sarge" a solitary voice replied.

Selby took this opportunity to offer round his cigarettes. After we all had a lung full of smoke and the tea had arrived, Sgt: Nichols blew his nose then turned back to DI. Selby. "Yer see Inspector they're mostly young lads, God bless 'em, seem to think they have let us down in some way" he now glanced directly at me "well I don't know" he continued "it's like I keep telling the silly little buggers, we all thought that in the last bloody shindig" he sighed. I gave him a half smile. "Look at the first go we had at the bloody Somme for Christ sake. Some twenty thousand men copped it at the first bloody rush". At this point Selby raised his hand "Yes Sergeant we do know, Sgt: Auger and I were part of that mad dash" Dave kicked in "and I'm afraid it's something none of us will ever forget" he promptly added. There followed a short pause "Anyway" Dave continued "the powers that be reckon with our boys flooding back like this, we must be diligent and guard against jerry sneaking in one or two of their own, just to keep us lot on our bloody toes, do you understand Sergeant?" Dave said. Sgt: Nichols seemed slightly stunned by this revelation, but nevertheless quickly jumped in with "Oh no don't you worry on that score Sir, we've all been warned to keep an eye out for them bloody termites. I doubt any will get by here Sir" he assured us with a knowing smile. Dave nodded, gulped down the last of his tea, he then shook hands with the Sergeant, said "Good, I'm glad to hear that Sergeant" and drew my attention to the fact that we were about to leave. Sgt: Nichols turned to me, shook my hand saying "Good luck in your search, hope you catch the bastards" I gave him a friendly smile then obediently followed my leader out through the door, down the steps and into the waiting car.

*

Dick Fletcher now wearing a medium grey suit handed over the stipulated sum of money that Mrs: Davies, his new landlady, required in advance to secure a room for one months' lodging. He had explained to her that he needed a permanent address as he was expecting his call up papers at any time now. He also added it would be nice to have a place to come home to when on leave. Mrs: Davies had in turn said she understood and promised she would always hold one room spare just for him. "Well that's very nice of you Mrs: Davies, I must say" he offered his gratitude in a sincere manner. "Oh, there's no need for thanks, and by the way my name is Sally" she replied. "Right, well in that case Sally, my name is Richard," he said as he started patting his pockets as though searching for something. He then suddenly turned back to her "I wonder if you would excuse me Sally, I seem to have run right out of cigarettes, I'll just pop out and get some" he said offering her a manly smile. "That's alright dearie, I'll make us a nice cuppa when you get back" she promised.

Now as Dick Fletcher walked along Warlingham High Street, it began to dawn on him just how lucky he had been in the last couple of days. His first stroke of luck came when he met a fresh-faced tanker driver and decided to hitch a ride with him from Folkestone. The petrol tanker driver happened to be sitting next to him in Big Harry's café on the Folkestone high street, and overheard him ordering one slice of toast and a mug of tea without sugar and milk and overheard him mention to a waitress, that he was waiting for the RAF to send him his calling up papers. Therefore he would like to get to Warlingham as soon as possible, so he would be near to Biggin Hill, where he knew most of the new intake of men start their training, and that's when the second stroke of luck came his way. The tanker driver, nicknamed Red on account of his mop of bright red hair, told him in strict confidence that he could give him a lift to Warlingham which was, as Red explained, just a few miles from Biggin Hill, where he was due to deliver his next load. So later true to his word, Red had dropped him off in Warlingham High Street, after telling him where a very sociable landlady named Mrs: Davies would no doubt have a room for rent.

8:

A WELL KEPT SECRET

Hornchurch, a quiet little country village right out in the sticks, and there we were Dave and me, five o'clock in the afternoon, and the bloody siren is blasting off a bleedin' warning again. "Ol' jerry must hate this little village Dave" I remarked as we entered that old shack they call a police station. "I don't know why" Dave grimaced. "Anyway just as long as they don't bomb the bloody place while we're 'ere" Dave offered with a smile. "Ah, don't put the bleedin' mockers on it mate" I sighed. It was then I suddenly received a hefty clump on my back which very nearly knocked me off my bloody feet. The blow was delivered by a big man that came up behind me. "Well I'll be buggered, how are you doing my old mate" a voice behind me wanted to know. On straightening myself up, I knew the voice, it came from the past. Nevertheless I had to wait a second or two for my teeth to settle back in place before turning round.

He still stood about six feet three inches but looked a stronger man. However the moment I set eyes on him, that terrifying Somme battlefield began replaying in my mind, and I clearly remembered this man Johnny Wakeman. When I was in hospital he handed me back my rifle 'Florrie May' that I'd lost during that battle, when I was wounded. I immediately grabbed his hand "Well blow me over backwards, look who it ain't" I almost sobbed with emotion. Selby stopped, looked at me, then to Johnny, suddenly recognition slid across his face. He threw an arm around the big man and with obvious emotion welling up inside him croaked "So them buggers didn't get you either son".

A long silence followed while the three of us stood staring at each other, then Johnny said "I'll be buggered" then Selby and me repeated his words "I'll be buggered". It took time for the emotion to subside in all three of us, but suddenly we were all speaking at once. I was asking 'how he had fared at Delville Wood' he was enquiring about Selby's arm, while at the same time Selby was reminding us about poor old Plumpkin. It was then all the chattering stopped. Silence returned once more, then I said with a lump stuck firmly in my throat "We saw the silly sod go down in a shell hole, and that was it". "Yes, we all did, but I heard fritz picked him up sometime later" Johnny volunteered. "Well I bloody well 'ope so" Selby put in effectively closing the subject. The silence returned. A lone voice from a side door said "Oh you're back then Sir" of course, it was dear old DC Tony Willis. Inspector Selby had decided to leave the DC behind while we took a quick trip to Folkestone. "Ah Willis," Selby called over, "anything new turned up yet?" "No not much, the Romford Superintendent wants to know if you have had a look at Suttons school yet Sir?" DC Willis informed us. Ins: Selby shook his head "Right Willis, we'll go down there next, you'll do the driving this time though" Selby informed him. He then turned back to Johnny Wakeman "What you doin' down 'ere anyway John?" he softly enquired. "I've been ordered to report to a Superintendent John Jarvis" he just managed to say before me and Selby came back at him with "Orders to report, who the bleedin' 'ell you workin' for then?" we both said in unison. However, Johnny just touched the side of his nose with his forefinger, and with a shake of his head whispered, "Sorry boys, no can say". "Oh, so you're one of them are yer?" Dave said pulling a strange face. I winked at Dave and told him "I know who 'e's workin' for Dave, 'e's one of them bleedin' undercover boys, who don't 'ave a sodden clue where to look for them saboteurs we've been sent out to track down". John Wakeman gave me a quick smile "You know Billy, they always said you were a clever little bugger" he replied as he made for the door. Then looking back at us raised a hand to his mouth and said softly "Remember though mums the word, see you later," after which he slipped through the door like a shadow. My old mate Selby looked over at me "There yer go Bill, we're all searchin' for the buggers now" he announced. "Seems like yer right Dave" I confirmed then added "what's our next move mate?" "I don't really know, let's 'ave a butchers at this bloody Suttons school they keep on about". He then called over "Willis out 'ere!"

On arriving at the school we found jerry had preceded us. Dave therefore instructed DC Willis to drive straight into the airfield which was only a few yards further along the same road, and it would seem jerry had selected this exact moment to drop in for tea. As it turned out the first two bloody bombs very nearly blew our bloody car through the sodden gates of the airfield, but like the brave proud riflemen we'd always been, nothing stood in our way. Selby and yours truly were out of the bloody car like a couple of jack rabbits, and into one of the slip trenches the airmen had prepared around here for just such an emergency. And that was before DC Willis had even stopped the bloody car. When Willis joined us in the slip trench, he smiled at me and said "Funny that Sir, I was going to suggest we left the car and hop into one of these Sir" he made the remark sound very much like he was taking the mickey. Ins: Selby gave him a stern look yet ignored the remark. I on the other hand offered what I thought to be a great case in our defence. "Well yer see Tony me ol' mate, Dave and me 'ave played this bleedin' game before, a few years back against the same bloody team would you believe, and of course our lot wasn't ready again, and fritz seemed to be a bloody sight quicker off the mark than us". There I rested my case. Tony looked back at me with a cockeyed grin lurking on his face. "Oh Sarge I do feel sorry for you poor old sods from that last bleedin' lot, but come on, the truth is you didn't really finish the bleedin' job, did yer?" he argued for the prosecution. "Well that's as may be mate, but now I suggest you youngsters stop criticizing us old boys and get stuck in, see if you lot can do any better, at least we showed yer 'ow it's bloody done" I rattled off. At this point DC Tony Willis capitulated and ducked further down into our little sanctuary as one or two of the enemy aircraft began to rake the field with machine gun fire.

"Oh for Christ sake, where's my 'Florrie May'?" I yelled while shaking my fist at the enemy aircraft. I vaguely heard Dave chuckle, then explain to DC Willis "Florrie May was old Billy Boys rifle, but I'm afraid that was in another day and age" then for me he added "so forget it Bill, let's just wait it out".

At this point it became painfully clear jerry had caught our boys on the bleeding hop, we couldn't see one British fighter in the bleeding sky. However we did spot several airmen from the ground staff fart arsing about, trying to operate some old dilapidated Vickers machine gun. For a time there I toyed with the idea of rushing over, and help show the silly sods how to handle the bleeding thing. But DI Selby advised against this saying "Look Bill, you can't run around doing that sort of thing now, you're too bloody old for a start. Anyway I doubt you'd be able to handle the bloody gun the way these boys have to now. I mean, look at them bloody Stuka dive bombers" Dave went on "not like those Eindeckers or Albatros eighty-odd miles an hour, these buggers are coming at you something like two hundred plus miles an hour" he finally concluded. "Well I must say, thank you for that great show of confidence Sir" I replied sarcastically.

Jerry tormented us for another half hour before terminating his visit with us. He then treated us to one final burst of machine gun fire after which he left. Nevertheless all this action gave DC Willis and myself enough time to smoke two cigarettes. DI Selby declined a second cigarette on account of his health, so he said. Anyway I don't know about DC Willis, but for Selby and me I'm sure it would be right to say we climbed out of that small slip trench with a feeling of nostalgia, joy or pleasure, call it what you will, nevertheless it's the same feeling you get after charging over the top and suddenly finding yourself safely in the enemy trench with the enemy gone. Although I must say standing in that bloody trench did also bring back a lot of horrific memories to me. I wondered for instance if poor old Sgt: Banks was up there looking over 'his boys' as he used to call us. "Never mind Banksy me ol' mate, we'll all be together again one day" I mumbled. Dave said, "Speak up Bill wot d'yer say?" "Ah nothing mate, just thinking out loud," I told him. "Right, well you just pop over there and tell them dozy buggers in that bloody office who we are, and you might also mention nobody challenged us on our way in, and find out who's in bloody charge Bill" Dave ordered while pointing to a shack that looked as though it was the orderly room. "You might also mention we're 'ere investigatin' complaints about people photographing their bloody airfield, just in case any of the buggers in there are interested" he called after me. I waved my hand in acknowledgement as I went. However, before I'd gone too far, Dave called me back, "'Ang on Bill, change of plan, no point in 'anging round 'ere, I've 'ad a bleedin' enough of this. Jump in we'll go back to the station".

9:

STRIKE ONE

Suddenly a Squadron Leader jumped from the cab of a three-ton lorry and ordered the guard on the Biggin Hill aerodrome to open the gates. A jeep and a brand new Bren gun carrier accompanied the lorry. As the gates opened the jeep revved hard on the engine then swung out in front of the lorry and entered through the gates first. Two men occupied the jeep, a RAF Sgt: James Freeman driving and a flight Sgt: Tom Henry as passenger. The Sqn: Leader slid back into his seat on the lorry, telling the driver to follow the jeep which Cpl: Todd, his driver, acknowledged with a nod and a crisp "Sir". Quite suddenly Cpl: Fred Todd and Sqn: Leader Bob Taylor became aware that something was drastically wrong with the jeep now picking up speed in front of them. First, Flt: Sgt: Tom Henry stood up and was seen to be gesticulating to the jeep's driver, it appeared something to their front was forcing them off the dirt track and the Flt: Sgt: seemed to be suggesting they avoid it. He next turned to the lorry and shouted what appeared to be some sort of warning to the lorry driver Cpl: Todd. The Sergeant then took a premeditated leap, out and away from the jeep. Sqn: Leader Bob Taylor having taken heed of the drama going on in the jeep immediately instructed Cpl: Todd to take evasive action "Swing out onto the bloody grass, clear of that bloody jeep" he yelled. However, a sudden explosion just behind the jeep had the effect of causing Cpl: Todd to automatically throw himself to one side in the cab, in an effort to avoid fragments of glass penetrating his face from the lorry's windscreen, when and if the blast struck. This in turn caused him to throw the vehicle into a sharp U-turn at the same time stalling the engine. Sgt: Ray Locke of the army's Royal Engineers driving the Bren gun carrier: the last vehicle of this small convoy, did not see all what went on in front owing to the three tonna blocking his view, but now Sgt Locke watched in horror as the lorry suddenly darted forward, went into a U turn and stalled just a few yards in front of him. He immediately pushed his foot down hard on the accelerator while applying a sharp lock to his right track. As the carrier slowed with its left track spinning freely, it went into a laborious turn, avoiding a collision with the lorry, but in order to prevent his Bren gun carrier from stalling he quickly reversed his lock on the steering wheel. Unfortunately, he was too slow taking his foot off the throttle, consequently now with steering wheel straight, the Bren gun carrier with army Sgt: Ray Locke at the wheel cursing, jumped forward with a rush. The Sergeant quickly slammed his foot down hard on the clutch, threw the gears into neutral, released the clutch then immediately slammed it down again, and finally eased the engine into third gear. He repeated the foresaid of doubling the clutch until finally bringing the carrier to a standstill without actually stalling the engine.

Meanwhile in the hedgerow of an adjoining field, Dick Fletcher, now dressed in an RAF uniform bearing the rank of Corporal, crouched down in a small hollow watching anxiously through a pair of field glasses which hung around his neck. Seeing a Sergeant in the jeep, suddenly jump to his feet and wave his arms about, seeming to be in some distress, at one time pointing to something on the dirt track in front of them. The sight brought a smile to the face of the corporal in the hedge. He continued to observe this little pantomime as the Sergeant in the jeep, pointed back at the lorry, shouted something inaudible then gave a gigantic leap and rolled well away from the vehicle. The RAF Cpl: first saw then heard an explosion come from the jeep. It seemed to lift this four-wheeled drive vehicle and throw it backwards just off the dirt track.

However, it wasn't until the man in the hedgerow, Cpl: Fletcher, saw the three-ton lorry jackknife and the Bren gun carrier career across the field that he began to curse himself for not planting a couple more landmines in the vicinity where the carrier had left the dirt track. Nevertheless he knew it was no good crying over spilt milk. He took one more peek through the field glasses at the tragic scene which he had created, then decided it was time to go. After replacing the glasses in their case and going to great pains to brush himself down, removing all debris from his spotless blue uniform, he walked over to a small gate, where he carefully removed his bicycle from its hiding place then carefully concealed the binoculars in the saddlebag. He then purposely mounted his bicycle and started a pleasant ride to Biggin Hill aerodrome, which assured him of a ride that would last at least five minutes!

Having arrived at the airfield, he waited for the Sergeant of the guard to order an airman to raise the barrier bar. Sgt: Blake then engaged him in conversation. "Hey Dick, where the bleeding hell you been? We've had the bleedin' devil to pay round 'ere" he told Cpl: Dick Fletcher. "Well hang on Sergeant, it was supposed to be my day off, anyway what's happened here then?" Cpl: Fletcher enquired showing mild interest. "What happened! look, leave your old bike over there, we'll take care of it" he promised while pointing to a place Fletcher should park his bike. He continued "then nip along to the orderly room, them blokes will know more about it than us" Sgt:

Blake concluded. "Right Sarge" came a somewhat puzzled reply. At the orderly room Fletcher was told by an airman what had happened "Only one sergeant killed though, which was lucky" he was informed. Fletcher answered "Who, for him? Bloody fortunate that" then inwardly bestowed several curses on himself for not laying more mines. Nevertheless he realised there was nothing he could do except learn from that silly mistake.

Later that day Cpl: Fletcher picked up his bike from its nesting place alongside the guardhouse. He told Sgt: Blake he'd be back in the morning. He did not envisage however, his stay at this airfield would be so short. Nevertheless he felt he could take comfort from the fact that two days ago, while supposedly helping the driver of a petrol tanker unload, had contrived to plant a small bomb in the empty petrol tank, which he was later given to understand exploded that same night on the other side of an adjoining field, well away from the airfield. So, he thought at least I can console myself with the knowledge that I've completely destroyed one jeep and a Sergeant driver, one petrol tanker and driver plus caused a lot of bloody havoc into the bargain, "not too bad for one night's work" he told himself.

*

I handed DI Selby a cigarette, as we both lit up he said, "Right Billy me boy, we'll 'ave breakfast now, then over to that bloody shack, their excuse for a police station around 'ere". "There you go then" I replied as I handed him a plate containing two slices of fried bread, two eggs and a couple of slices of tinned spam. "Thanks," he smiled then added, "What you got?" "Oh me, I'm trying that new prefangled powdered egg, them yanks keep sending over for us poor old Englishmen to live on, with some good old British toast thrown in" I informed him. Now having settled down to eat our first meal in our new abode, I took time out for a casual observation of our new surroundings. The décor wasn't too exciting, just plain apple green distempered walls which some idiot had gone to great lengths to brighten up with some fashionable dado. This room I assumed was the dining room, on account of a sideboard that stood against one wall and contained the cutlery, also the table we now sat at boasted a set of four chairs to match, a tablecloth and all the other condiments that are required at meal times.

At this point my keen eye and sharp mind were distracted by the ringing of a telephone that was placed on a small table in the hallway. I looked at Selby with the same look he was offering back at me. "Ah me ol' pal, one of us 'as got to answer that bloody thing, and it ain't gonna be me, on account I'm still eatin' and you're the senior bleedin' partner in this small team anyway" I very shrewdly pointed out to him. He took a huge bite of his fried bread and mumbled something which sounded like 'it's probably for the clever one of us, so you stay put while I give whoever it is a nice bollickin'. He then slipped out through the door.

I forgot about studying our surroundings and concentrated on this make-believe egg that our American friends reckoned would do us the world of good, although as it turned out I only had time to devour one more mouthful before DI. Selby was back. "Come on Billy Boy time to go" he managed to inform me, then my leader was gone. By the time I caught up with him Selby had already knocked on the front door of DC Willis' digs and was waiting for some response.

Quite suddenly our Wolseley slid quietly curb side. A head popped out through a front window "Are you looking for me Sir?" DC Willis sang out in a happy go lucky tone with a wave of his hand, and a big smile covering his face. I walked closer to Selby then nodded to Willis who by this time had the car back doors open and stood waiting. "He's 'ad a sight more than a good nights' sleep and a nice English breakfast, I'll wager Dave" I speculated with a touch of envy. "No, not so soon, surely," Selby muttered, then with a touch of doubt added, "d'yer reckon Bill?" I gave Dave a knowing smile "Yes Dave I reckon," I replied and gaud blimey as if to confirm what I'd just said, Willis' young landlady opened the front door and stepped out. The wind caught her dressing gown, and from where we were now sitting an awful lot of leg came into view as the bottom half of the gown parted, then not only did she wave to Selby and me, she finished her goodbyes by making a great exhibition of throwing a kiss to DC Willis which he immediately returned with interest. "There yer go Dave, what did I say," I reminded Selby. "Well I don't know he must have some bleedin' spell he can cast over these lovely women" Dave replied.

On our arrival at the Hornchurch police station DI Selby received a smart and courteous nod from the desk Sergeant. "I think Mr: Daniel Ross wants to speak with you Ins: Selby" the Sergeant informed Selby. "Ah right, and you are Sergeant?" Selby waited. "Oh yes Sir, I'm Sgt: Wright Sir" he enlightened Selby. "Ok, that's good, thank you Sergeant" Selby gave out in a dismissive manner, then turning to me "so come on Bill, where do we find this Ross feller? We'll go and see him immediately" Selby carried on. "Well, I should think he still lives at 22a, Stanley Road Dave," I told him with a hint of despair in my voice while rubbing my backside and remembering that bloody gate with its new spring.

This time I held the gate firmly until Dave and myself were safely inside, then I gently closed it. And that's when that snotty nose little bundle of joy came flying out of the house which stood opposite and yelled to his mates something almost undecipherable "Yere, yerry yup yelse we'll be late" then without waiting for an answer was off legging it down the road. However, my supersonic brain had deciphered his message before dear old Danny had opened his front door. What the snotty nose bugger had said was 'Here, hurry up or else we'll be late', so problem solved.

Danny shook Selby's hand and indicated that Dave should go on through into the front room where we had conducted our last interview. I too stepped through the front door and like Dave shook hands with dear old Danny, I also enquired after his health. He assured me there was no problem there. So I moved passed him and followed DI. Selby into Danny's front room. Suddenly I sensed something was wrong, the hairs on the back of my neck stood up, I made to pull away from the open door, but what felt like a hand in the centre of my back propelled me uncontrollably forward through the door, and there laying on the floor was poor old Dave: my chief, my ex sergeant, my mentor, my friend, the one I'd looked up to all these years, well I had to really you see, the bugger had always been taller than me! Anyway, one thing I can vouch for, when someone bangs you over the head with a bloody sledgehammer, you really do see stars. I know this for a fact because the devious bastard who'd been hiding behind the door, had very nearly knocked my head off with one. Believe it or not, I actually stood for a moment and counted three bloody stars before sinking to my knees and letting my nose caress the floor.

10:

A VISIT TO LONDON

Cpl: Fletcher now lying on the bed in his Warlingham lodging house, was trying to calculate how much damage he could cause by taking a trip into London, and perhaps placing a few booby traps around one or two small factories in and around the London area. After some consideration he considered it a good idea. All he had to do now he decided, was to sort out which factories would be worthy of his attention, and of course which would be the easiest factory to infiltrate, and hopefully cause the enemy a great deal of damage. After laying there for an hour or so longer, he decided he would first return to the Biggin Hill air base and put in for a weekend pass. That, he reasoned would give him two full days in which he could select suitable targets, in say places like Stratford or Bow, where he knew for instance the Bryant and May match factory stood, all be it, a cock stretch from Bow Road tube station and positioned in the Old Ford Road, presenting no problem at all. He therefore decided he would stay on at Biggin Hill and use it as his base for the time being. Having at this point made up his mind, Dick Fletcher removed himself from the bed and engaged in a quick shave and brush up. Knowing that Sally, his landlady, had just recently pressed his best uniform, he therefore thought it would be a good idea to slip into said uniform and present himself to the orderly room where he could request a weekend pass, after which he could return to his lodgings where he would then confirm one way or the other whether Sally his landlady was in fact a sympathiser. After all she had within the last couple of days given him every indication this was so. He further surmised that Himmler himself had connived for her to be on hand in case of emergency. That being the case, he silently praised the SS Furher for some good thinking.

*

I woke to the sound of a soothing voice cooing "Come on Sgt: Auger, wake up now, you're alright, come on open your eyes" So just to be awkward I opened one eye to take a peek at whoever this was pestering me. What I saw with that one eye made me immediately open the other eye in double quick time, and when I say this nurse was beautiful, it's a lie, coz she was absolutely gorgeous. "Why didn't you wake me sooner?" I complained. "My dear Sergeant, I've been trying to wake you for about half an hour" she politely told me. "Right, well I'll let you off this time, but do try harder next time" I returned. She simply stuck her nose in the air and walked away from me, with my eyes following her every move, while my mind jumped back remembering the time I'd woke up in a Belgium hospital, surrounded by so many beautiful young nurses and an exceedingly desirable sister, who I judged to be in her thirties and at the time much too old for me. What a naïve bloody idiot I must have been.

My gorgeous nurse returned, this time however with a small trolley trailing along behind her. "I'll just check make sure your brain is still functioning Sergeant, so just sit back and relax" she instructed. "Right" I replied. "Ok Sgt: Auger, follow my finger with your eyes side to side, up, now down, yes everything seems alright there" she announced, "now let me just take another peek at your wound" she next ventured. Of course, while this was going on I could do no more than admire a beautiful heart-shaped face, surrounded by a mop of shining fair hair which was, I hasten to add, half-concealed under a bloody *tin hat*! 'wow' I thought, it's coming to something when Billy Auger starts chatting up nurses wearing a bloody tin hat, I just couldn't believe it. Never mind, she still had a good pair of shapely legs, and besides I was really enjoying myself now with my face nestled into the hollow between her perky pair of breasts, while this lovely nurse examined the wound I had received on the back of my barnet. "How does that feel?" she asked. "Oh wonderful" I replied snuggling in a little closer. "Does it hurt there?" she next enquired while pressing with one finger down the back of my head. "Oh no, that's great nurse" I assured her at the same time realising I was giving all the wrong answers. Anyway that's when my old friend DI Selby put his head around the door and asked, "How is he nurse?" "I think he's good for a year or two yet Inspector" she replied. She gently pushed my head away, gave me a wicked smile and a sly wink, which inferred there could be more to follow.

DC Willis arrived and told us the car was ready and waiting outside. The silly sod never gave me a bleedin' chance to ask my nurse her name, still I suppose I shouldn't go on about that really, after all I am a married man, and my little nurse Florrie May is still as lovely as ever. Anyway, as we stepped through the Oldchurch hospital front door, it suddenly occurred to both Selby and myself that with each of us now wearing a nice clean white bandage around our barnets, and with a great deal of serious rain now pouring down, we would soon be looking like a couple of drowned rats. Nevertheless once again DC Willis saved the day when he produced two umbrellas, so now with each of us holding tightly to a brolly, we made a mad dash for the car, and tripped arse over tip down a bloody high curb in the process! Selby ended his excursion lying full length in the road, while yours truly brazenly kissed the back door of the highly polished car, and of course our brilliant dash for the car still left us looking like a couple of bloody drowned rats.

However it wasn't until we were approaching a place called Roneo Corner just outside Romford that DC Willis revealed that at the same time Selby and me had been nobbled, dear old Danny Ross had been murdered. "What!" Selby exclaimed, "do you mean while Sgt: Auger and me were lying there after being clobbered, the bastard then murdered that poor old bugger Ross!" Selby barked in an outrageous tone. "'Ow'd the poor sod get it?" I quickly broke in. "Well whoever it was, used the same method he'd used when clobbering yous two, which must have been something like a cricket or baseball bat or something bloody similar, hard to tell really" Willis revealed hesitantly. Silence rained for a few moments. Then breaking the short pause he added "Anyway the forensic people think that's how it was" he concluded. "Right, so the forensics are there now, I take it" Selby said quietly. "That's right" Willis sung out. "And I take it the silly sods 'ave removed the body?" Selby next asked. "I really couldn't say" came a spontaneous reply. I could see our leader DI. Selby was now in deep thought, so I calmly tried in my most eloquent way to throw a lighter note on the subject. "Ah, don't matter if they 'ave Dave, they will 'ave taken photos of the crime scene and you will see pictures of a dead body with a bloody gash in 'is 'ead" I stated. Dave gave me a long glance, then a smile broke out on his face. "There you are Willis, see 'ow simple it is" he told the DC and quite suddenly burst into a fit of laughter. "See" I said with a smile. But suddenly Dave's laughing ceased, and another question was bouncing around the car. It would seem this time Selby was now doing his best to put our skills of deduction to the ultimate test, his question was "Everyone keeps saying 'he' killed poor old Danny Ross, but 'ow the bloody 'ell do we know it was just the one?" The question was posed in such a way as though to offer a challenge. DC Willis at the wheel shrugged and gave Dave a quick glance. I offered what I thought to be a better scenario with "Perhaps there's three or four of the buggers around Hornchurch Dave, then what?" I smiled. "Then What, Yer silly sod, then we're in a bleedin' lot of trouble, and that's a fact!" Dave replied as we bumped along in the Wolseley.

11:

A MATCH TO BRIGHTEN THINGS UP

Having finally established his landlady Sally was still a firm Nazi supporter, who had in fact gone to great lengths in order to persuade a tanker driver named Red to keep a watchful eye out for Cpl: Fletcher, and make sure he was on hand when the Corporal needed a lift out of Folkestone. Red had very cleverly conspired to fulfil this task, and practically delivered the Corporal on to Sally's doorstep. So now with no more niggling little doubts about his landlady, Dick Fletcher boarded a district line train and arrived at Bow Road underground station at about mid-day on the Friday. Having previously arranged to stay at the Romford YMCA, he now thought it a good idea to spend the Friday afternoon just strolling around this part of London, making sure he knew exactly where to place any small gift he might feel inclined to leave for the night workers, just to make life a touch more exciting for them. He also thought that by surveying the Old Ford Road area in daylight, would be a sight better than fumbling about at night in these fruitless blackouts the British persisted on. It would for a start give him Friday night and all day Saturday to put one or two things together, which he hoped the workers in the Bryant and May match factory for instance, would appreciate.

Cpl: Fletcher had already contacted the YMCA just outside Romford, and been assured they were holding a room for him for Friday and Saturday night. He in turn had promised to vacate the room by mid-day Sunday seeing as the long weekend pass he'd been granted, was due to expire at 10.00pm Sunday evening. He reasoned that this should give him plenty of time in which to place a few surprises around the Old Ford Road area. After all, from what he could see, the Luftwaffe hadn't even touched this part of London so far. He therefore reasoned that by creating a little mischief in and around Bow Road itself and the Old Ford Road in particular, he would then be assured of causing a great deal of havoc plus putting a great deal more fear into the local inhabitants, which could no doubt deprive the night workers of their daytime sleep. This in itself may eventually cause one or two careless mistakes amongst the night workers, and could lead to certain individuals nipping out in the dark for a quick fag, in order to overcome their tiredness and calm their nerves, where they would through tiredness, inevitably forget to follow the blackout rules, by first striking a match in an open doorway where possibly a glass window adorned an adjoining door, and without knowing it, the reflection of the lit match would be seen for miles around. Then of course, the culprit would then go parading around the factory grounds puffing away on the cigarette, not realising that the light from just one quick fag could clearly be seen by any observant Luftwaffe pilot from near on 10,000ft above. This then was the result Cpl: Fletcher was hoping for as he made his way to Romford's YMCA, where he was to enjoy a typical wartime meal, after which he had a quiet brandy and ginger with a Sergeant from the RA regiment, then after making his excuses retired for the night.

Now alone in his room Cpl: Fletcher lay on his bed and began to work out the exact ingredients he would need to cause an explosion or perhaps a fire. After giving the matter some deep thought, he considered the best option would be to start a fire from whatever flammable material was on hand. 'Yes' he thought 'that would be the wisest thing to do'. It was at that point Fletcher remembered how as kids, they were able to set fire to some old dried up leaves, by first placing two or three red top match heads in between two bolts which were then held together by a nut in the middle. Then it became a hit or miss exercise placed squarely in the laps of the Gods. It was just a matter of throwing this homemade contraption amongst the selected material and hope that when it struck the ground it would ignite. He decided this to be a far better option than trying to rack his brain in conjuring up some materials for a homemade bomb, after all this would without doubt mean he'd be obliged to visit one or two chemists for said materials and in all probability, having signed for them, would create an added danger of his face being remembered by the chemist. This then, he reasoned eliminated the bomb option for the time being. As quickly as he had discarded the bomb idea, another idea took its place.

A smile slid across his face, and his fertile mind wandered back to the old fashion torch trick which is quite easy to put into action. All that is needed, a torch with good batteries, and in this case perhaps one house brick or a mound of earth, in fact anything to make the torch stand upright pointing towards the sky. It didn't have to throw a particularly bright light, just enough to catch the eye of a Luftwaffe pilot, maybe even a Stuka dive bomber pilot as he goes into the attacking dive. Of course, the more he thought about it, the more he realised that one or even two torches would not suffice. No, what was needed, he surmised, must be at least half a dozen torches, and they must be placed in various concealed positions in a wide circle around the target to be bombed, also in such a way as not to attract the attention of one of those ARP men, who go around at night shouting "Put that bloody light out". Although he thought, in this case an ARP man could very well be of some help, simply because while busy calling for people to put a light out in a house, these men were not looking for a small light, say in someone's back garden, or maybe closer to a target. So this then was Cpl: Fletchers last thoughts before slipping between the sheets and drifting off for a full eight hours undisturbed sleep.

By eight o'clock next morning, the Corporal was up, washed, shaved and halfway through breakfast, when for no reason in particular he took time out to glance around this immaculately laid out YMCA dining hall. On doing so his eyes took in several photos of famous people caressing the walls, such as Billy Bishop, the American 1st World War Ace fighter pilot, next one of Amy Johnson, then adorning the opposite wall a portrait of Winston Churchill. It was at that point the German saboteur became prey to a coughing spasm, which suddenly turned into a full-blown outburst of laughter that even prodded a nearby soldier into enquiring after the Corporals health.

The whole episode was brought about, he realised, simply because on seeing the Churchill photo, his mind had quickly jumped back to Heir Himmlers office and the painting he'd seen there of Hitler. As it happened, at that very moment while the bogus RAF man had studied Churchill's photo, he had suddenly become aware of the flaw in the Fuhrers painting. It exhibited the signature of a not too well known Jewish artist, who had changed his name from Saul Solomon to Karl Schmitt, which it would seem every German except the Fuhrer knew. After composing himself the Corporal offered his apologies to the other guests, then left the hall.

*

As we walked into the Hornchurch Police Station, a very smart uniformed police Sergeant held up his hand "Hang on a minute gents, are you Inspector Selby and party?" he enquired. "That's right me ol' cock" Selby answered. "Good, well we've just been informed by some Doctor from the Oldchurch Hospital, that you Sir and your Sergeant must rest for at least forty eight hours," the sergeant said as though fulfilling a life's ambition. "Yes, well that maybe so, my good sergeant, but then we've just been informed by the Super himself, that there's no need for rest, work is the only answer for a quick recovery. So there you are my good sergeant, the Doctor must 'ave it wrong" Selby recited back to him with a smile. "Up to you Sir" the sergeant mumbled, then wandered off. Selby turned to me and was about to speak when quite suddenly we heard a raised voice slipping through the thin walls. "No, no, I'm saying you can't do that" the first voice shouted. "Oh no, well you just stand there and bloody watch me mate" the second voice threw back aggressively. "It sounds as though we're all in the same bloody room, what with these walls only being stuck together with plywood, I daresay every bugger in the station can 'ear them," I told Selby. However, it was dear old Dave himself who put into words what I was thinking. "That bloody voice sounds familiar Bill" he offered. I cocked my head to one side to listen further. "Yer know Dave, if I didn't know any different, I'd say that was bleedin'". At that point my summation was cut short by a long low rumbling fart, which seemed to bounce from wall to wall in the old wooden shack, then just fade away into silence. "That bloody well is 'im Bill" Selby yelled as we both rushed for the door. "It can't be" I sung out on grabbing the door handle and slinging the door wide open, which of course created a situation neither of us were prepared for. Kneeling on the floor in front of us, there appeared an old lady scrubbing the floor. Scrubbing brush and soap in her hand, bucket of water at her side. So in order to avoid this unexpected booby trap, Dave veered to the right, inadvertently catching his foot on the edge of the old lady's bucket, which tilted him backwards, leaving him sitting on his arse drenched by the bucket of soapy water. I very cleverly swerved to the left in order to avoid the woman and bucket, but to my surprise found myself sailing through the air, having run straight onto a wet soapy floor. My airborne excursion came to a jolting end with me lying spread-eagled on my back, looking up at none other than dear old Plumpkin, my long lost army pal, who we'd thought we'd lost in Delville Wood in 1916.

After kindly helping me to my feet, my long lost friend had a go at me for rushing through an open door like some bloody school boy, or words to that affect. Then before we'd been given a chance to ask, he hurried into a tale of how he'd been lost in Delville Wood some twenty-four years previously. "What happened" he began "was you lot ran down into a bloody gully, but me soppy sod I was so engrossed watching to see where the bloody 'ell you lot would all come out, and of course I wasn't paying attention to where I was bloody going. On trying to dodge round a shell hole, would you believe, I slipped and the bloody 'ole swallered me up. I ended at the bottom with two big bleedin' Germans for company, the buggers stayed with me all the way back to a bleedin' Boche prison camp. So there, that's my bloody story" Plumpkin rattled off in double-quick time. Selby and I just stood there dumbfounded. "Well I'll be buggered" I put in at length, then Selby chipped in with "Ah, that accounts for why we couldn't find you. Me and Bill 'ere searched every inch of that bloody wood". "Yeah, we see yer go down, but couldn't find no trace of you anywhere, so naturally after that, we assumed the worse" I added with a shrug. Plumpkin stared at me for a moment, then his gaze turned to Selby. "So yer came 'ome, joined the bloody police force and completely forgot about yer ol' mate I suppose" Plumpkin complained. "No, not at all me ol' mate, 'avin' this job means we can from time to time make discreet enquiries," I tried reassuring him. Then for no reason at all added, "Of course we 'aven't bothered lately". Plumpkin's face parted in a wide grin. "Oh, I see, thank you very much" his words danced back to me. That's when all the hugging, laughing and back-slapping began.

We offered our sincere apologies to the poor old cleaning lady. Selby I noticed slipped her a one-pound note, and ordered a constable to help the old girl get reorganised. After giving Plumpkin our address and directions on how to get there, I told him he could call on us any night for a drink. Now with DC Willis accompanying us, with the both of us still nursing sore heads and still sporting a clean white bandage each around our barnets, we were driven by Willis round the corner to the Stanley Road crime scene.

12:

A FRUITFUL NIGHT

By the time the bogus Cpl: Fletcher stepped off the District line train at Bow Road underground railway station, he was beginning to feel the twinge of butterflies fluttering about in the pit of his stomach. However, he realised this was a sure sign of an adrenalin rush, which could only have been brought about by the forthcoming events he was looking forward to putting into action. Having obtained six medium-size torches from the YMCA and placing them in a small briefcase, along with two boxes of Swan Vestas red top matches, plus twenty Woodbines, all accompanied by a couple of large jars of Brylcreem that famed hair cream which the RAF boys favour, and consequently led to them being tagged with the mantle of the Brylcreem boys. Neatly hidden in each jar was two medium-size bolts with a nut to fit. The Corporal handed his ticket to a lady porter, at the same time enquiring if he could board a train from here directly through to Dagenham and was sharply told 'yes, from the opposite platform'.

The corporal going into the role of saboteur hurried from Bow station, headed straight across the main road, graciously waited while a mounted constable walked his horse out through the police station stables gate and down onto the main road, which would eventually take man and horse parallel with the Mile End Waste market.

After negotiating his way through and clear of Tom Thumbs Arch, he next found himself in Tredegar Road.

Then the bogus RAF corporal immediately started cursing furiously on realising he was now completely lost, which left him no option but to enquire from a passing police officer exactly where the Old Ford Road was situated. The policeman eyed the RAF corporal with lingering suspicion, then eventually said "Well now, this 'ere is Tredegar Road, now if yer go straight on down to your right, yer should pass Parnell Road on your left, keep going past Fairfield Road which will be to your right, then Old Ford Road will be straight in front of yer" the policeman concluded while still eyeing the bogus corporal with obvious suspicion. "Thank you officer" the corporal replied with a friendly smile and was grateful the officer asked no questions of him. However, once alone he began to have doubts, by asking for directions he had openly compromised himself. So should he for instance have tried to lure the policeman away to somewhere quiet and somehow silenced him, but then of course, that would have presented him with the problem of disposing of a body in broad daylight, or alternatively he could postpone this operation and wait for another time. Although for a moment at one point it seemed as though the policeman showed signs of suspicion, Fletcher nevertheless chose to disregard this policeman's attitude because in his experience police forces of every nation suffer with the same suspicious affliction. So he simply ignored this up-keeper of the law's attitude and concentrated on his forthcoming evening's work.

*

As it transpired it took Constable Len Taylor exactly eight and a half minutes from Tredegar Road to the Bow Road police station. He at once reported on a suspicious character he had encountered and engaged in conversation, and was convinced the man was up to no good. A description of said man, and where he was most likely to be found was sent to all stations.

On entering 22a, Stanley Road this time, both Selby and I were a great deal more cautious. We examined each room of the property in turn. Of course as DI. Selby had surmised, the body of Daniel Ross had already been removed from the crime scene. Nevertheless two constables remained on duty guarding the premises. One of these constables had made a point of obtaining photos of the crime scene from the Laboratory, he handed them to Selby, alas they were of a limited amount of value to us.

However, his mate whose name was Ken Charles, put forward quite an interesting theory when he suggested that Danny Ross was in fact himself an enemy agent, and the sole purpose for him being here, had been to mislead the Essex police into thinking that the Hornchurch aerodrome was the enemies prime target. Up till now he'd served his purpose very well. At this point Constable Ken Charles was cut short by a tap on the door, which swiftly opened and a head with a tin hat stuck on it whipped around the door jam, and a voice sung out "DI. Selby and your Sergeant are wanted urgently back at the station by the Super". Selby looked at me, raised one eyebrow, I smiled back at him, and announced, "Must be bloody serious Dave". To which he answered with a quick nod back at me, then turning to officer Charles said, "Thanks officer for your enlightenment on the subject, very interesting, I will keep you in mind young man". After which we both departed.

Back at the Police Station Dave stated "Yer know Bill it wouldn't surprise me if that PC. Charles has got the whole bloody thing sewn up". To which I could only agree. Anyway as we walked on through the station Dave was handed a note by a very smartly dressed sergeant, which turned out to be from the superintendent himself, and read as follows 'DI. Selby, you and Sgt: Auger must leave immediately for Bow Police Station, this is an urgent request from Bow, so be sharp about it' at the bottom of the message was scribbled the signature of the Romford's Assistant Chief Constable Richard Allan. After reading the note, Selby folded it and stuffed it in his coat pocket, then said "Right Bill, we won't 'ang about 'ere. We'll 'ave lover boy Willis drive us to the train station, catch a train straight through to Bow" he rattled off. Once in the car he added to Willis "right me ol' dream boat, the railway station quick as yer bloody can". DC. Tony Willis responded with "Right Sir". On entering the station Selby told DC Willis to return the car to the Police Station car park, then catch a later train and join up with us at Bow Police Station. "Will do Sir" Willis replied before giving us a friendly wave as he drove away.

*

After spending Saturday afternoon in Victoria Park, and now settled on an inconspicuous park bench, the bogus RAF Corporal assured himself that all the torches contained new batteries and could be relied upon to last at least forty eight hours, which would include one complete night. Having completed this task he moved on to his next devious device. He removed the nuts and bolts from each jar of Brylcreem, made sure they were both wiped clean of any excessive cream, he then placed four red match tops into a rather large nut, then carefully screwed a matching bolt either end, making sure to leave a hairs width of space between match head and bolts, so that when the contraption hit the ground, it automatically forced the bolts to ignite the match heads, which in turn would cause a small flame which may hopefully cause a large fire.

Now with everything tucked away safely in his briefcase, the saboteur began a nice easy stroll to the Old Ford Road. Nevertheless, he realised the match factory lay further away from the few shops situated in the middle of Old Ford Road, so therefore it would be just as easy for him to cut into the Old Ford Road at the park end, and on into the Roman Road by way of Parnell Road, then through to Tredegar Road and cut back out onto the other end of Old Ford Road. However as it happened, after some twenty minutes walking, he found himself in Clayhall Road where he stopped just long enough to ascertain exactly where the Old Ford Road was now situated. On further investigation, he discovered by simply crossing over at the end of Clayhall Road, he then in fact would be standing in the Old Ford Road, but now at the far end, in other words just five minutes walk from the Bryant & May factory, his prime target.

13:

LATE AGAIN

DI. Selby and I had an agonising three and a half minute wait on Hornchurch station before a straight through train from Upminster to Bow appeared. We made ourselves comfortable in the first carriage, both relaxing with a cigarette. "'Aven't got a bloody clue what this is all about Bill, any ideas mate?" Selby enquired as the train rattled through the dusk of evening on its way to Bow. "Well according to the grapevine Dave, apparently some copper spoke to a fella in Bow who he reckoned was a bit dodgy, and the description he gave of this bloke matches that of the bugger we're looking for" I Informed a puzzled DI. Selby. This statement resulted in Dave blowing two perfect smoke rings in my direction, Dave shook his head and mumbled "Yer know Bill, this bleedin' case gets more complicated each bleedin' day". Two more smoke rings drifted my way. He gave the subject a moment's thought, another smoke ring floated towards me. I coughed and fanned away the smoke signals that were dancing about in front of me. He then leant forward "It makes yer wonder just who the bloody 'ell we're 'unting for," he growled, then glared straight at me and added, "You got any bloody idea who it is?" I silently shook my head "If I knew mate we wouldn't be lookin' for the bugger now" I replied after a moment.

As the train pulled into Plaistow station we sat waiting for the doors to open. I suddenly realised it was one of the older trains we were now on, so jumping to my feet I rushed over and opened the bloody door myself to get a drop of fresh air before the train went underground, then immediately heard the blast of an air raid warning. I at once slammed the door shut, walked back to my seat and moaned to Dave. "There yer are mate back in bleedin' London, and we've walked straight into another bloody bomb display by ol' fritz. Would yer believe!"

*

It took the bogus RAF corporal roughly five minutes to discover Spring Street and Summer Street which just lay off the Old Ford Road, practically opposite Clayhall Road. As he entered Spring Street a piece of waste ground presented itself. He quickly positioned two of his torches, which were angled in such a way as to be hidden from the sight of the residents in Springs and the adjoining Summer Street, yet still directed towards the Bryant & May match factory. He then moved on, decided to leave the Old Ford bus station, instead he crossed over the road, slipped smartly into the gate of an adjoining factory, which apparently produced round cardboard milk bottle tops, where he very cleverly arranged two more torches, once again slightly angled toward Bryant & May. Once satisfied, he stealthily negotiated his way through the Bryant & May gates and there quickly scraped a small hole in the ground, switched on one torch, planted it halfway down the hole, and painstakingly smoothed the earth around it. This one however, he had made sure to position in an upward stance. He then quickly nipped out of the gate back onto the Old Ford Road, only this time heading in the opposite direction towards Tredegar Road. On turning into Tredegar Road he hopped over a small fence belonging to the first house, where he found an ideal spot to position his final torch, which once again he directed towards Bryant & May. In the distance he could now hear the first wailing of an air raid siren, so hurried on to the Bow Road underground where he boarded a half-empty train for Upminster.

*

We arrived at Bow twenty minutes after leaving Plaistow. The reason for the long delay we put down to the number of times the bloody train stopped, in order to let enemy aircraft clear the area, because the flashes caused by the electric line could be clearly seen by enemy aircraft. Anyway by the time Dave and I nipped out of Bow Station, dashed across the Mile End Road and crashed through the police stations heavy door, I reckoned at least ten bloody bombs had exploded nearby, and with so many anti-aircraft guns in action and dozens of bloody searchlights bouncing around the sky, we were as you can imagine only too grateful to reach the sanctuary of the big safe building.

Once inside the station, we found half of the bloody Bow constabulary mingling about in the stable yard, all watching our searchlights as they tried to lock onto one of the enemy aircraft, without too much bloody luck, I might add. These officers seemed to have no bloody fear of all the bombs and shrapnel from shells that were jumping about in abundance, but suddenly a voice in pure cockney yelled "Oi, you two new blokes from Hornchurch, yer wanted in 'ere, look bleedin' sharp". Selby and I both turned to see if we could discover which of the numerous back doors this bloody voice had come from. We finally pinpointed it as the door that lead off a narrow corridor which followed into a row of holding cells. "Blimey, he sounds like a bloody 'appy bugger Bill," Dave said with a smile, while standing to one side to allow me to go first. I declined to answer or to accept his offer, instead I bowed and indicated that he as the senior officer should lead the way. "Thank you, you bleedin' peasant," he told me with a friendly dig in my belly.

On arriving at the front desk, Dave enquired of the desk sergeant "Who was doing all that bloody shouting about two blokes from Hornchurch wanted bleedin' sharp?" The desk sergeant stood up straight, head high, but his face went as red as a beetroot. "Ah, yes well, I'm sorry about that Sir, but it was the Super you see, he told me to say 'Tell them buggers to look bleedin' sharp'," there DI Selby cut him short with a wave of his hand "That's alright sergeant, just tell me why the rush?" he asked in a friendly tone. The sergeant, relaxed slightly, yet still looked uncomfortable. "Oh, well the reason for that Sir is because Constable Taylor has been told to hang around until you got here Sir, and explain to you exactly what he can about this RAF corporal he spoke to earlier today in Tredegar Road" the sergeant informed Selby. "Ah, now I see Sergeant, so where is this officer Taylor?" Selby enquired. "Yes well as to that Sir, you should find him four doors down, just on your right, along there Sir," he said, at the same time indicating which door he meant. "Ok, right thanks Sergeant," Selby began, then after a short silence he turned to me and continued, "look Bill, you cut along, see what this Taylor bloke has to say for 'imself, while I'll nip." Whatever else Dave was about to say both me and the desk sergeant would never know, because at that very moment all the back doors of the station flew open, and for a second or two there was complete silence. Suddenly a gale-force wind, which after knocking the three of us off our feet, seemed to sweep through each room in the building, there then followed the loudest explosion I've heard since that Somme fiasco in 1916. Anyway Dave bounced to his feet like a rubber ball "You two alright?" he quickly asked, then instantly added "that one landed amongst them silly sods out in the stable yard". Having made this morbid statement Dave darted through one of the now wide open back doors, the sergeant and I closely behind him.

However, what we expected to see was in complete contrast to what we actually did see. For apart from the fact that one or two of these amateur aircraft spotters were now standing about with one hand covering one ear everything seemed perfectly normal. That is, if you can call searchlights dancing across the sky, anti-aircraft guns doing their best to ruin the ozone layer, and bombs jumping about everywhere, normal. I turned to the sergeant "Why are them silly sods 'oldin' their ears?" I enquired in puzzlement, but before the sergeant could speak Dave answered my question. "Well that's bloody obvious yer dopey diner, yer see them silly bleeders copped the blast in that ear they're 'oldin', when the bloody bomb exploded" he enlightened me in his usual confident manner, in an effort to make me look twice the fool I was! "Oh I see" I meekly replied. Dave shook his head in despair "never mind Bill, some of us know and some don't" he told me. He then went on to say "That really was weird though, I could 'ave sworn that last bomb exploded out 'ere in the yard". Seeing as he was senior partner in our team I simply agreed with him as usual, then he started in once again "anyway Bill let's go see what officer Taylor has to say"

As it happened what Taylor told us sent me and Dave rushing out of the Bow police station down towards the Old Ford Road. On account of him saying he believed this dodgy RAF corporal was down there, to amongst other things cause some mischief in the vicinity of the Old Ford Road area, and of course my parents still lived in Old Ford. So, like the two ex-riflemen and London detectives we were, and now are, we both went as shadows through the night.

14:

GRANDMA SUSPECTS GAS

As it turned out, on our arrival in Old Ford we could see at once that although part of the place had been obliterated by the nights bombing, so far the cockney spirit was still prevalent. Most of the men while helping those people who had survived the Summer Street bombing, were at the same time venting their anger at the jerry Luftwaffe. It was in fact one of these old boys that handed a torch, which was in good condition, to Selby saying he'd found it in a garden in Spring Street which was opposite Summer Street. He reckoned this rather strange, as it was still switched on and seemed to be angled towards Bryant & May match factory. Dave and I also thought it rather strange, especially when someone else placed another torch in Dave's hand, telling us he'd found it in Bryant & May itself and like its twin brother still switched on, only this one had been positioned in an upright position. This fellow also told us a bomb had exploded in the yard of the match factory, blowing a steamroller or something very similar over into some old lady's front yard.

Of course by this time we'd been round to check my parents were alright, they both turned up trumps, still light on their feet. My old dad was in fact busy explaining to the old boy, who owned the barber shop next door, how earlier that night, an aerial torpedo dipped over from the back, then climbed up the back wall, sailed over the roof and away without exploding. It was at this point another old fellow who ran the tobacconist, the other side of my parents, chimed in saying he'd been told that first a parachute had wrapped itself around one of the match factory's towers (chimney) with a land mine swinging, still attached, and secondly it wasn't a bomb that obliterated Summer Street, it was in fact rumoured a bloody land mine had floated onto it, so he was told.

Anyway me and Dave left it there, we wandered back to the carnage of Summer Street and to hopefully find the old girl who was having trouble with a steamroller. On our way, we first passed a fish and chip shop on our left, then a pub on the corner, on passed a small cul-de-sac which seemed to lead into a bus station of sorts. There were even out of service buses parked both sides of the road. On crossing this road we were next confronted by a small detached house which seemed to stand out on its own, surrounded by a rather large picket fence and sure enough, there smack in the middle of a small front yard snug tight under the only front window we could see downstairs, lay some sort of steamroller. "Blimey Bill that must 'ave given the ol' girl a bleedin' 'eart attack," Dave sung out. I just nodded and immediately started banging on the old girl's front door, while calling in a pleasant a voice that I could "Open the door luv, we're 'ere to 'elp yer". Dave also chimed in with "Come on mother you'll be alright, open the door dear". No response came back at us. Nevertheless while we were doing all this serenading we became aware of a great deal of steam still expiring from the contraption stuck under the old girl's window. Funnily enough though, from where we stood we could see the sodden thing hadn't touched any part of the picket fence. So it must have been blown straight up over the Bryant & May wire fence, and somehow sailed across the road then dropped straight down into the old girls front yard, without touching the fence or any part of the house for that matter.

Quite suddenly there came a muffled voice which was barely audible above the hissing of the escaping steam "The keys on a bleedin' string in the letterbox, yer pair of dimwits" it told us in a beautiful old cockney tongue. Anyway it was Dave who eventually retrieved the key from inside the letterbox, this of course was a habit most Londoners would practice in those days. By hanging their spare key inside the letterbox, it meant they would never lock themselves out and in the case of an emergency a neighbour or close friend would be able to help if necessary, and this in fact was what Dave and I were endeavouring to do, but instead were making a right balls-up of a job.

So now with Dave in front of me, it automatically gave him the honour of opening the door, where we knew this old cockney lady would be shaking with fear. At least that's what we thought. However we were both brought up short when we entered the room, because there seated on a chair next to a table that was positioned under the bay window an old girl sat glaring at us. She had what we perceived to be, some sort of scarf held up in front of her face, and although the room smelt musty, there was also a strong smell of urine floating around the room. On the table lay a small bowl half-filled with water, next to it a bag of sweets with a snuff box close by. "What on earth are you doin' mother?" DI. Selby asked in amazement, and at that point tried stifling a fit of giggling. I also seeing the funny side of it was doing likewise. Anyway for an answer he received a lingering hard stare. Of course dear old granny must have sussed what we were thinking, for this dear old cockney lady sneered at us "Yes well the pair of you may snigger, but I'm a rememberin' the last bloody war, and in the manual I received it clearly stated 'in case of gas, place a rag soaked in urine over yer nose and mouth, so there" this poor mislead creature quoted this snippet of useless information as though it had come straight from the bible. "Oh no Gran that's no good, 'aven't yer got a government-issued gas mask?" Selby enquired in despair. "Yes of course I've got one, it's upstairs under me bleedin' bed alongside me piss pot" she answered, then shaking her head added, "but it was a sight bloody easier to pee in me drawers, whip 'em off and 'old 'em over me face" she proudly admitted, and before either of us could utter another word she went on "anyway, you say it's no good, but it's bloody well asaved me," she announced. "No, no, my darlin' it's not gas, it's steam you can see" I gently informed her. She glared back at me in amazement. "Not one of them bleedin' gas bombs they used in the last lot, you say?" I smiled and shook my head slightly. "No gran" I assured her. "Oh well, in that case I'll 'ave another toffee," she told us on perking up "An' you two can make a pot of tea" then she grabbed the bag of sweets which lay beside her on the table "D'yer want one?" she offered. We both declined a toffee and tea and headed towards the front door, promising to send around a local bobby to check and see she was alright. "Oi, make sure the bleedin' keys still there" the dear old thing requested as we closed the front door and burst into laughter.

Now as we started to retrace our steps towards Bryant & May a soft voice cut through the dark "Ah there you are Sir," and of course Selby and I knew at once we were now in the presence of that lady's man DC Tony Willis our driver and the third member of our team. "Where the bleedin' 'ell you been?" Selby warmly greeted him. "Well Sir, the train stopped for over half an hour just outside Barking for a bloody start" Willis began, at this point Selby raised his hand "I know, don't bother, say no more son, you ran into an air raid, so the bloody thing had to wait till it was all clear, is that right?" Selby put forward for Willis's defence. "Spot on Sir" Willis readily agreed. "Right then, until I say otherwise, yer stick with us, 'ave yer got that son?" Selby demanded. "Loud and clear Sir". DC. Willis replied as we all three groped along through the bloody blackout.

When we finally arrived at Bryant & Mays gate Selby put into words what I'd been thinking "Look lads, there's bugger all we can do 'ere, the sod we're after 'as obviously been and gone, I daresay he planted them bleedin' torches then bloody scarpered, and us silly sods ain't got a poxy clue as to where, so let's get back to the station" Selby recited. "Seems to me all we've done tonight is quash gran'mas' fears about the bloody gas" I put in. Then DC. Willis added a few words which could not be heard on account of a police car that tore past clanging its bell for all it was worth. "Wonder if them idiots can see where the bleedin' 'ell they're goin'" I vented my thoughts. "I'd like to know who they're after, tearin' around these dark streets like that?" Selby enquired. "Yeah, and with no bleedin' lights on either" Willis added for good measure. "Still we mustn't condemn 'em too much, after all they are on our team" I pointed out. "Yeah but rushin' about like that, they could quite easily kill some poor sod" Willis put in the pot.

It was then DI. Selby stepped in with his prediction "Yer know boys in years to come everybody will be flyin' about in one of them bloody death traps, and no matter where you may live all yer bleedin' neighbours will 'ave two or three of them tin boxes stuck outside their bleedin' 'ouse, you just mark my words" he very wisely and patiently informed us. "Yer mean them silly sods won't be content livin' in a bleedin' brick box and goin' to their grave in a wooden box, they'll wanna spend the in-between bit runnin' around in a tin box. Oh 'ow bleedin' excitin'," Willis chuckled.

15:

MURDERERS ROW

The bogus RAF corporal Dick Fletcher handed his rail ticket to a collector at the Hornchurch railway station, who showed not the slightest interest or suspicion when the corporal enquired as to which direction the Hornchurch aerodrome lay. The man took his ticket, smiled and said, "New are you son?" The corporal smiled back, then replied "Does it show mate?" and went on "there's a sight more new blokes on the way". "Blimey they must have lost quite a few boys then" the ticket man surmised with a shake of his head. "Anyway" he continued "you turn right out of the station here, then keep on going straight down pass the school on your right" he then hesitated for a moment, produced a pen from his pocket and grabbed a sheet of paper off a desk which stood just inside his little office. "Here, hang on a minute, I'll write it down for you" he volunteered. "That's very kind of you" the RAF corporal thanked him. "Ah that's alright corporal, we very often have to direct the new ones" the porter replied as he studied the sheet of paper he now held in his hand. However he did not pass the paper to Cpl: Fletcher straight away "See, I've marked it here" he pointed with his pen "now there's the school 'Suttons' it's called" he then waited a second or two before handing his written directions to the patiently waiting corporal, after which he took a tin of tobacco out of his pocket, measured a two-inch strip into a fag paper then started to roll a very substantial cigarette. On its completion he tucked this new creation comfortably behind his ear, re-arranged his peak cap then referred back to the sheet of paper that he'd handed to Corporal Fletcher with his artwork proudly displayed and said "As you can see I've put a cross where the school is, so like I said go on pass that and you'll find the airfield waiting for you on your right" again he paused, then added "really all you have to do is keep going and looking to your right, you'll eventually wind up on the airfield, and it shouldn't take you too long because you're not carrying much kit I see". The corporal held up his briefcase, tapped it with his hand and said "All I need is in here, anyway thank you very much for your help" he added and with a final smile turned and made his way from the station.

*

When we finally arrived back at Bow Police Station some thoughtful young copper supplied us with a mug of hot tea, and a plate loaded with digestive biscuits. We neglected to ask where so many biscuits had come from. "Ah just what the doctor ordered" Selby declared while rubbing his hands together. "Where we off to next Dave?" I asked with a mouthful of biscuit. "Well to be honest Bill, I've got this gut feeling that tells me the bugger we're chasing about after will no doubt be 'eading for Hornchurch about now" the inspector paused for a moment, looked very thoughtful before continuing, "although come to think of it" at this point the inspector broke off again, gave me and DC. Willis one of his long in-depth glances, then burst out "yeah, of course that's it Dagenham, there's Fords and Briggs, there's also one or two other factories down there the bugger could go for". He left it there, jumped to his feet, gulped back a long mouthful of tea, stuffed a biscuit in his mouth and mumbled something that sounded like "let's get bloody moving". "Sod it, another bloody train ride in the bleedin' dark" Willis complained.

As we crossed the road from police station to railway station, DI. Selby put into words my thoughts "Well at least one things for sure, ol' Superintendent Rickman was right, bleedin' jerry did slip a few of their lot in with our boys at Dunkirk, them bloody torches verify that alright, what yer reckon Bill?" he confided. "Yeah me ol' mate, I've been thinkin' that all along" I offered as redress. Next it was Willis's turn, he presented the obvious which Dave and myself had purposely neglected to mention "The question is 'ow many of them buggers got through?" he smugly enquired. "That constable is anybody's guess," Selby told him.

We climbed aboard the third carriage of an Upminster train just as two young soldiers from the Fusiliers hopped off and immediately went into a routine of chatting to a couple of over made up, under-dressed young females, while we guardians of the law looked on with envy. Selby rolled his eyes with a deep sigh "I don't know, youngsters today!" he remarked with a touch of disapproval in his voice. "Ah never mind 'ere 'ave a fag" Willis chuckled as he offered his pack of Senior Service. It was then for some reason or other my mind slipped back in time and I remembered Sgt: Johnson back in the last war giving Rifleman Topley a bollocking for trying to have it off with a young French girl up against an old barn. I smiled to myself at this memory, then immediately tried to erase the incident clear from my mind as sadly both men involved were later killed in action.

However while I'd been wrestling with past events, Dave had obviously indulged in some deep thinking of his own. He suddenly jumped to his feet "'Ang about lads, on second thoughts now we know for certain its either one or two krouts we're lookin' for, I'm not too sure he or they would be rushin' down to Hornchurch or Dagenham after all" his words came rattling out at us sharp and fast, machine gun fashion. "Whoa 'old yer 'orses Dave, I think yer can be sure it's just the one bugger we're dealin' with 'ere, and guess what, I've got a gut feelin' we've 'ad dealings with this particular sod in the distant past" I quickly fired back at him. DC. Willis stood mouth open, he first looked at me then at Dave, and I saw his eyes roll upwards. Dave came back at me "What the bloody 'ell you on about, dealin' with 'im before?" Dave groaned and looked puzzled. "Oh for Christ sake, remember the captain on the white 'orse, the Somme?" I jogged his memory. His face lit up, nodded his head and came back with a long drawn out "Of course".

It was then the train started moving, going from Bow towards Bromley. The silence between us seemed to float around the carriage for a minute or so, it then fell to Willis as junior member of our team to inform us we were on the move. "So gentlemen its either Hornchurch or Dagenham now" he declared as he exhaled a lungful of smoke, pinched out his half-smoked cigarette, tucked what remained into his right- hand dog end pocket of his coat and quickly added, "besides I ain't got any bloody idea what yous two are on about". This final declaration brought an end to DC. Willis's thoughts on the subject. He then sat down folding his arms and closed his eyes. I grinned at Dave "Now what?" I offered in despair. "Well what I'm thinkin' Bill, the bugger could 'ave decided to stay in London after all" he paused for a moment, grimaced gave a slight shake of his head "in other words the sods outwitted us again, he knew bloody well us silly sods would go runnin' back to Hornchurch thinkin' he'd head straight for that bloody airfield, but instead the clever bastards stuck around London, after all there's them bleedin' blocks of flats in Hackney for a start, and that's not to mention all them underground stations 'ereabouts, Jesus he could 'ave a bloody field day" Dave once again rattled off in a torrent of passion. "Yeah, and 'ere we are all doin' what he bloody well expects, brilliant" Willis put in for good measure. Next it was my turn "No Dave the people from them flats will all be down their air raid shelters," I cleverly pointed out. "Yeah but all their bloody 'omes will be gone," he very smartly offered in return. "No ol' jerry won't see them bleedin' flats, remember the blackout," I reminded him. "Blackout, bollocks, when did that ever stop 'em?" he next wanted to know. To that I could give no answer, so I quickly changed the subject "and besides, bombing them underground stations won't do much good, they're bleedin' bomb-proof, that's why they cut the electric off at night and whole families sleep down there in safety all bleedin' night" I mentioned this as though passing on a state secret. "Yeah well we all know that mate, but what about if a couple of them bombs bring the whole station down on top of 'em" Dave paused for a moment, gave me a look that made me start thinking about what he was hinting at. He continued "they'll be a few bleedin' 'eart attacks before they can dig too many of 'em out, I'm tellin' yer Bill" Dave concluded as our train crept to a stop in Bromley station.

There followed a loud hissing sound, the doors slid smoothly open. Suddenly a few dim lights that still glowed in the carriage went out. We found ourselves in complete darkness. DI. Selby was on his feet again "Now what?" he started. A voice on a loudspeaker cut him short, "Everyone please leave the train, please vacate this train and take immediate cover, there is a violent air raid in progress.

At this time anybody who happened to be in the vicinity would have seen three brave officers of the law sprinting hell-bent for leather from train to platform and onto the street, do a quick turn right down the Bromley Hill, passed the cemetery, also situated on the right, straight into the nearest community street brick built air-raid shelter, without once stopping for a breather. When we eventually settled down in this newly built shelter, we noticed six pairs of eyes glaring at us with deep interest. One old boy reached over and raised the wick in an old trench lantern, so now we could put faces with the eyes of our six cell mates. Two men and four women came clearly into view, all middle-aged. The old fellow who'd raised the wick in the lamp gave us a courteous nod, stuck a pipe in his mouth, sat back on the long bench, folded his arms then studied us some more. The four old girls were all busy knitting, although they still found time to give us the once over. Their companion, the second male in this small congregation, after satisfying himself that we were actually specimens of the human race, stuck a fag in his mouth lit it and commenced blowing great volumes of smoke everywhere, he then leant forward and started to write what I presumed was a love letter to some young bird the poor old sod had tucked away somewhere or other.

We vacated our chosen place of safety just after the all clear had sounded round about five am. DI. Selby then suggested going back to Bow Road, after all they should be able to hand out a mug of tea, he reasoned. "Yeah and who knows they might even throw in a slice of stale bread toasted" DC. Willis put in hopefully. In actual fact we each received two slices of toast. Having enjoyed the small offering, DC. Willis and myself relaxed with a cigarette while Dave Selby was once again obliged to spend time visiting the Superintendent.

On his return Dave announced we were all going on a tour of East London. First stop is Bucks Row, from there Hanbury Street then on to Bemer Street or to be more precise Dutfields Yard, we will next pay a call on Mitre Square. It was there I held my hand up to silence him "'alf a mo Dave, you're takin' us on a bloody tour of murderers row 'ere, I suppose we also pop into see Mary Kelly at 9, Millers Court then, to finish the tour," I proposed. "Yer know Bill that's exactly right, yer see, some bright spark back at the yard thinks one of them murdered ladies was related to a German family and our boy could be 'anging around 'ere abouts somewhere. Mind you I do believe they've changed some of the names of the streets, anyway you're right, it's as yer say Bill, a walk back down memory lane into Murderers Row," he concluded.

16:

A NEVER ENDING ARGUMENT

After taking a quick look at the Hornchurch airfield and making a note that only a six foot fence separated school from airfield, the bogus RAF Corporal, Dick Fletcher, decided he would have a wander around the Hornchurch village, which he considered to be a far better idea than just hanging around the airfield and trying to cripple a spitfire or two on the airstrip with his so far untouched fire bolts. He reasoned he could then perhaps sort out a target in the village itself. So now with these two unused devices still reposing comfortably in his briefcase, he retraced his steps only this time going towards the village.

Leaving the aerodrome and walking back pass the railway station then going on straight down passed an old shack advertised as a police station, at the same time bearing round to his left, negotiating a small slope which took him into what he guessed was the centre of this quiet little village. His reasoning for this was based on the fact that he now stood outside a pub called 'The White Hart' which was situated on what looked to him like an island with three major roads running around it. The corporal entered this old village pub with trepidation, but to his surprise quickly found the locals eagerly plying him with half pints of English ale. He could only guess at the reason for their generosity to be on account of the RAF uniform he wore. Nevertheless Cpl: Fletcher made a point of only staying with one half-pint while at various times passing others onto other men in uniform.

It was however at one point, while handing a newly arrived young bus driver one of his unsolicited half pints of ale, that he overheard the bus drivers' companion saying "Oh yes, apparently two policemen were knocked unconscious and the owner of the house was murdered". "Jesus that was bleeding dicey wasn't it?" the bus driver declared, after thanking a generous RAF corporal for a half-pint of ale. "Well they're saying the culprit was a bleeding spy who killed him" the informer concluded.

On hearing these few words the bogus RAF man decided it was time he left this small village. Not wanting to return by way of the local railway station on account of maybe running into the ticket collector, who would no doubt be full of awkward questions. To avoid all this he decided to enquire of the bus driver for the best alternative way to catch a train to London, without walking back up that bloody hill to the Hornchurch station. "Oh that's bloody easy mate, just hop on an 86a bus over the road there" the driver pointed to a bus stop through the pub window "There see, takes you to Upminster Bridge Station, jump off there, stations right opposite" he was eagerly told by this friendly bus driver. The corporal then shook hands with one or two of his new found friends, gave a thumbs-up sign, a mock salute, and left.

*

"As far as we know ol' Jacky boy only disposed of five prostitutes and they all lived within a mile or two of each other, believe it or not, and yet in 1888 he had several hundreds to choose from" DI. Selby enlightened us on beginning our walking tour of London's East End. "Yer know I could never understand why they didn't get the bugger's prints" DC. Willis said out of the blue. Selby glanced at me "Yer know my son that would 'ave been a good idea, but it wasn't until 1901 that Sir Edward Henry in India worked it out, then the English police adopted the system. Mind you, there must 'ave been any amount of fingerprints left at each crime scene, although at that time, we didn't 'ave the expertise to process them anyway" my dear old friend cleverly observed, however me like a clown had to have my two penneth and walked straight into dangerous argumentative territory. "I wonder just 'ow many innocent men been 'ung on the evidence of fingerprints?" I mockingly enquired. Dave threw me a glance that said 'idiot'. DC. Willis gave out with an offbeat cough. I looked from one to the other "What?" I declared. "Well mate, you a Detective Sergeant an' yer don't even know fingerprints are considered infallible? No two people 'ave the same bloody prints, every bleedin' idiot knows that" Selby growled with a friendly dig in my ribs, and that's when clever bollocks me, really put a spanner in the works "Ah, that's just it Dave, perhaps we are all bloody idiots at that, to believe it" I offered back. Dave glanced at DC. Willis and winked "'Ow d'yer make that out me ol' mate?" he asked as though speaking to a ten-year-old. Now it was my turn to look towards Willis, I gave him a grin. "Well yer might smile me ol' pal but listen 'ere, who says no two set of prints are the same?" Suddenly Dave burst out laughing "Yer silly bleedin' sod" he croaked through a fit of laughter. "No no 'ang on a minute Dave so why do they say it? Go on answer me that" I rattled off in one breath. "Well it's been tried and proven by experts, yer bloody dim wit" Dave reminded me. That's when I fired my big guns "yeah, that's exactly what I mean Dave 'experts', them bloody Generals that thought up the battle of the bleedin' Somme, wasn't they experts? So I still say 'ow many poor innocent buggers 'ave been 'ung on account of the sodden experts, who insist no two sets of prints are the same?" I broke off there. Selby had stopped walking in order to offer round his cigarettes, we then went through the ritual of lighting a cigarette, then DC Willis said through a cloud of smoke "Blimey Sarge you could be right at that". However DI. Selby was having none of it. "No me ol' mate, they're not idiots, they know what they're doin'" he replied in an unconvincing tone, then added two smoke rings to boost his argument. "Well they say that Dave because out of all the prints they've taken, they have yet to find two sets the same, anyway they couldn't possibly know until they've taken everybody's prints, So until they do" I left my argument there again and shrugged my shoulders, then nigh on choked my bleeding self, trying to blow one of Dave's decorative smoke rings.

"So what yer sayin' is, the experts 'ave got it all wrong" Dave smugly replied. "No what I'm sayin' me ol' mate is them so called experts are assuming no two sets of prints are the same, simply because they 'aven't come across two sets the same yet" I threw back with an equal amount of smugness and satisfaction. Dave stepped forward stretched out his hand and ruffled my hair. "Alright yer blonde bombshell, I don't agree but still, 'ave it your way" he finally capitulated. I pulled away straightening my hair "No, 'ang on Dave, think about it, we're only in this bleedin' war because of them so called experts" I added as my closing argument. "Christ all bloody mighty, you've lost me completely now, what are you on about Bill?" he growled back in amusement. At this point I decided to let it go, but DC. Willis took it a step further "Yer know I can see what yer mean now sarge, them bleedin' politicians they're all supposed to be experts at negotiating, ain't they?" he showed such poise and elegance in putting this argument forward that even I had to laugh. At this point DI. Selby with tears of laughter now running down his face, put an arm around each of our shoulders and guided all three of the cleverest detectives in Britain across the road. "Come on you pair of clowns, let's go and see if we can find ol' Jacks' ghost" he said gasping through fits of laughter. This of course cut off our debate instantly.

Way off in the distance we heard the first wailings of an air raid warning, and as we manoeuvred our way into JTR's old hunting ground, around the Whitechapel area, DC. Willis suddenly called out "What the bloody 'ells that?" and pointed to a building which seemed to be coming towards us. It did in fact take several seconds before any of us realised the front wall of the whole building was actually collapsing, and had we stayed where we were, three of the best police officers in Britain would have been buried alive. Fortunately for us DC. Willis's warning came just in time, although funnily enough it wasn't until best part of the building had collapsed that we heard the bloody bomb explode, and I'm sure I speak for all three of us when I say three very nervous men quickly vacated the scene. However on doing so we found ourselves in the wrong bloody street. Instead of going into Bucks Row where dear ol' Jack had left his first victim, Mary Anne Nicholls, no doubt because us highly intelligent guardians of the law had been involved in a heated discussion about fingerprints, DI. Selby had inadvertently taken us into Hanbury Street where of course Annie Chapman's body was found.

"Never mind we'll 'ave a quick shifty around 'ere, then move on to Bucks Row" he informed us, then a second or two later more or less, he repeated an earlier remark "Mind you it's like I said, since then they've changed the names of them bloody streets." DC. Willis and me nodded in agreement. I didn't really understand why we bothered to acknowledge, because by now everyone knew only to bloody well the street names had been altered ages ago.

Anyway we didn't have much time to dwell on the subject. As Selby opened his mouth to speak again, an open back lorry slowly edged its way into the middle of this narrow street, and with a pair of twin Pom Pom guns which were fitted on the back of said lorry, suddenly began to open fire furiously at a bothersome Junkers 88 Bomber which had been trapped in the beam of a searchlight. "Jesus where in God's name did they come from?" DC. Willis yelled in amazement as we all dithered about on the curb looking for somewhere to hide. "I don't know, but he's making enough bleedin' noise, wherever the bugger came from" Selby quickly replied. Just to let them know I was still with them I almost screamed above the noise of those bleedin' guns "Yeah and now ol' Jerry knows them guns are 'ere, he'll soon be comin' after 'em, so I suggest we take a bleedin' powder quick".

17:

A BREAKTHROUGH

Back at the Bow Road police station Dave Selby told me and DC. Willis to find somewhere to rest for a while. So after Willis had cadged a couple of cups of tea, we commandeered an empty holding cell to relax in. While sipping tea and puffing on a cigarette, which we must have been doing for about an hour, a uniformed sergeant came through the door and presented each of us with a plate of buttered toast. "'Ere boys you look like you need this," he said in a fatherly tone, while placing the plates side by side on a small chair. As we both offered our thanks to the sergeant, DI Selby popped his head around the cell door "I don't suppose you've got a slice or two left over sergeant?" he enquired in a hopeful way. The sergeant, who must have been a man rushing towards his 60th birthday, gave Dave a friendly smile "I think we can rustle up one or two more for you Sir" he answered slipping through the door.

Dave sat on the edge of a small table that had been secured to an old windowless wall opposite the door. He looked first at me, then at Willis, his face turned serious "Now look fellas we came 'ere in the first place hoping to find someone of German origin, you know, someone connected to the fatherland amongst these poor bloody retch's that Jackie boy obviously didn't like" Selby began, while both Willis and myself listened patiently as we knew only too well this would be a long drawn out recital "Well as it 'appens" he went on "it makes no bloody difference if there is a connection, because all we're interested in is catching the bleedin' bastard before 'e does worse than just leaving a few torches lying about for 'is mates to see. Now what I suggest, first thing in the morning you Tony, commandeer a car from the pool somewhere so we'll 'ave wheels, but before we do anything else, I want to pay that ol' girl in Old Ford another visit, coz I think we can learn one or two things from 'er. Right now get some rest, then it's up early tomorrow" he finally concluded. I of course asked him to repeat it on account I'd fallen asleep halfway through, he simply said "Bollocks".

So now it turns out all three of us were up, washed, shaved and dressed ready to face the world at 6am in the bloody morning. "Right, it's Old Ford Road first, see the lady who likes wearing a pair of peed in bloomers around 'er face" Dave smiled, giving his first order of the day. "Yeah and I can pop in see 'ow my folks are doin'" I put in for good measure. "Strange yer should say that Bill, coz I was about to suggest it" DI Selby informed me with a knowing grin.

As Dave and I walked through the yard of Bow police station we were obliged to wait by the stables gate, until DC. Willis could manoeuvre a black Wolseley car from around the back of a long-forgotten parking area, which had been designed some time ago no doubt to accommodate several police horse-drawn carriages. At length with the help of two or three police officers, he managed to negotiate this big black vehicle across the yard, past the horse stables and out through a side gate, straight onto an almost quiet street.

*

When Cpl: Fletcher finally stepped from the train at Whitechapel that morning, he considered spending a night on a British underground train in wartime, was something he would definitely not recommend to any of his fellow countrymen. It had appeared to him that every time an anti-aircraft gun had fired, the train would stop and wait for an hour to let the marauding aircraft clear the sky. They'd been through this ritual several times throughout the night simply because of the flashes thrown out from the live rail, which these electric lines constantly discharged, could give an enemy pilot a target to aim for.

The only consolation he could derive from this experience was the fact that he'd been travelling on one of the older trains, that allowed him to open a door for himself, and seeing as he'd been travelling in an empty carriage, he'd decided it to be a good time to dispose of his two childhood nut and bolt devices which still lay dormant in his briefcase. Making sure all lights in this lonely carriage were dimmed, he'd slowly opened one of the doors just enough to throw his first nut and bolt, which he quickly did, and was instantly rewarded with a bright flash followed by a dull thud. Apart from that nothing else happened, nevertheless he had achieved the satisfaction of knowing his childhood device still worked. He'd therefore decided to next rid himself of the second device. He'd disposed of this one through another door further down the carriage, but was sadly disappointed on not hearing a miniature explosion which should have followed. Instead what he'd heard was someone out of sight in the dark, probably a railway worker yell, "Fuck that" followed by complete silence. Cpl: Fletcher had quickly closed the carriage door, went back to his original seat, sat with his eyes closed, waiting patiently for the train to continue its journey. Of course he had no way of knowing that the railway worker would report the incident to the police, and also present them with the evidence.

*

On visiting my parents that morning, DI. Selby and myself learned ol' fritz had very seriously tried to destroy all the docks the previous night. Apparently the East India Docks "'Ad been delivered of bloody thousands of them bleedin' fire bombs (incendiary bombs)" was the way my dear old dad phrased the event. My mother, not to be outdone, told us that jerry had also had a go at St. Pauls Cathedral. "Look" she added "you can still see the fires" she pointed in the general direction, and sure enough at a quick glance we could see some thick smoke rising from around dear old St. Pauls, and that got me seriously thinking. I decided right there and then my mum and dad must move away from this bloody battle zone. It also struck me that Florrie May and I could do likewise, 'Yeah' I thought, we could all move in together, vacate London, start afresh, in Essex, maybe Dagenham or Romford, then again there's that quaint little old village called Hornchurch where they use a wooden shack for a police station. However all these plans had to be shelved for the time being, because at this moment DI: Selby along with DC: Willis was saying their goodbyes to my folks and urging me to join them.

Now finally we were able to pursue Dave Selby's quest to have another word with the old cockney lady, who believed peeing in her bloomers and covering her face with them would save her from being gassed. This time one knock and the old girl's door swung open. "Ah, I was aspectin' yous bleedin' lot" she greeted us. "Well that's worked out just right then mother" Dave informed her as all three of us entered the old girls front room. "'Ere yer 'ansome bugger, sit over there" she indicated a chair for DC: Willis. "Right thanks ma" the handsome sod replied. By now Dave had already grabbed a chair for himself, while I stood around thinking I'd probably end up sitting on the old girl's lap, "Ah now you, yer big bleedin' lumux, can sit yerself down on that little bugger of a stool, look over there, just beside that bleedin' ambitious pot plant. Bleedin' thing" her monologue stopped there for the time being as she treated herself to a pinch of snuff. She then took a big white handkerchief from her pinafore pocket and gave one gigantic sneeze into it, then, she continued where she left off. "Don't know whether it wants to live or die, like the rest of us silly sods" she turned to Selby "Now young man, what are yer awantin' of us thisa bleedin' time?" she put the question to Selby in pure old cockney, only this time with a touch of old Irish brogue thrown in. Dave gave her a big grin, but before he had a chance to speak I jumped in with "We've made this return trip especially for that cup of tea you offered us earlier mum" to which she quickly responded with "Oh, yer 'ave 'ave yer, well yer can make it yer bleedin' self, coz I ainna gonna move from this 'ere ableedin' chair, now then!" Now with a grin all over his face, DC: Willis hopped to his feet "I'll do it, where's the kettle?" he managed while still posing with a wide grin and trying desperately to hold back a fit of laughter, "With the rest of them bits and a-pieces bleedin' jerry left me with last night, in I daresay what's left of me bleedin' kitchen" She jerked her thumb to indicate the kitchen which was next door. She sighed then went on "An' will yer be-a-lookin' at that load of bleedin' junk them lazy buggers 'ave left me a-stuck out in me bleedin' front yard?"

I could see Dave was getting slightly impatient with all this small talk. He suddenly raised his hand "Yes right we'll see if we can get somethin' done about that, but in the meantime what we really came for my love, was to find out if yer can remember anythin' out of the ordinary that 'appened that night of the bombin'" he gently enquired, without, not for the first time I might add, coming straight to the point. "Well, what the bleedin' 'ell d'yer think 'appened? Them buggers were back again rearrangin' the fuckin' place" she flatly told him. "Yes I know all that mother, but did you notice anyone or anythin' out of the ordinary that day?" Dave finally got across. "Oh, yer should-av ask-us t'other day, there was that sodden git in the bleedin' airforce uniform, a-wanderin' around 'ere 'alf the bleedin' night. Thought no one could see 'im, but I was a-sittin' 'ere in the bleedin' dark, eatin' me bleedin' toffees and I asaw the bugger sneakin' into the ol' matchstick gate and sneakin' out agin" she thoughtfully revealed. That's when Dave jumped to his feet, grabbed both the old girls hands and kissed them with genuine affection "Thanks mother, you lovely lady, that's exactly what we wanted to 'ear, a man in RAF uniform you say?" Dave said in excitement.

18:

SWINGING AT AIR

AND JABBING AT SHADOWS

With only a pack of cigarettes and half a box of matches in his briefcase, the bogus RAF Cpl: Fletcher felt a good deal safer. After all he reasoned, he wasn't carrying anything incriminating, he could now relax a trifle and make his way back to Warlingham. He realised sooner or later of course, a change of uniform would be called for, but for all intents and purposes, this one must suffice for the time being. He had decided to hitch-hike a ride back to Warlingham, and luck was with him at his first attempt thumbing a lift. Sadly however his luck began to dwindle away when he jumped into the vehicle and found himself sitting next to an RAF Sergeant. After throwing his briefcase onto the back seat, he addressed the sergeant named Rowland "Hi sarge, nice car, what is it 'Vauxhall'?" he cheerfully enquired. "Yeah, it's one of their new efforts, anyway forget the bloody car, where the hell have you been Corporal?" he asked in not a too friendly tone. The bogus corporal stared back at him in utter surprise. "I had a weekend pass, sarge" he quickly explained. "Yes my old son, but that expired some time ago, and we've got people out looking everywhere for you" the sergeant admonished him. "Jesus Christ sergeant it's only been a few hours, and anyway I got stuck on a bloody train that kept stopping and starting because of the bombing, then I was entombed in an air-raid shelter for half the night" Cpl: Fletcher offered in his defence. "That's as maybe but you'll still be up in front of the old man tomorrow morning" he was warned. "Ah well, what will be will be as they say" the corporal relented, but inwardly he thought, somehow or other Sgt: Rowland must be disposed of, and the sooner the better.

*

Once back at Bow police station Dave sacrificed his last three cigarettes. We all lit up, then having opened and begun rummaging through a drawer in the desk of Assist: Chief Constable Allan's office, clever sod Dave suddenly stood back, waved a sheet of paper above his head "I've got it, 'ere it is" he sung out, then laying the paper on top of the desk, poked a finger at it "See Bill that's what we wanted, a connection; look there, on the same day Constable Taylor reported he had reason to converse with an RAF Corporal in Tredegar Road, well that same night our ol' girl saw a bloody RAF bloke creepin' about" Dave cheerfully presented his evidence. "Ah now I'm with yer mate" I'd finally cottoned on. "We now know who the bloody 'ell we're lookin' for, an RAF corporal" I happily passed on this information to DC. Willis, who just nodded and smiled. Dave happily blew two smoke rings my way, then said, "Right, where the bloody 'ell do we find this bugger?" "On a bleedin' aerodrome of course," I suggested.

*

It was when Sgt: Rowland drove by a recently bombed building that Cpl: Fletcher struck on what he considered to be a wonderful idea. His only problem he realised, was putting his idea into being. First, he must by some means have Sgt: Rowland stop the car. Once this had been achieved, second, he could make some excuse for opening the car boot, where he knew a large heavy spanner should be. So well on their way to Biggin Hill, Fletcher suddenly sung out "Christ sarge: I'm bursting for a slash, can we stop a minute?" "Hang on a second," the sergeant said, showing no sign of suspicion "Here will this do? nip behind those bushes over there" he instructed. Having spent a couple of minutes behind a bush, Cpl: Fletcher reappeared. "That's better," his voice rung out, smooth and clear. Sgt: Rowland now out of the car threw down an half-smoked cigarette. "Ready?" he called slipping back behind the steering wheel. "Yes Sarge" came the short answer, followed very quickly by "Hang on a second sarge, I think you've got a flat one here". Rowland wound down his window "What you on about corporal?" he called. By this time however the bogus corporal had opened said boot and was clutching a very large spanner. He called to Rowland "Don't worry sarge, I'll use this foot pump" no answer was forthcoming. So now satisfied the sergeant would just sit and wait, he began to manoeuvre silently alongside the drivers' side of the car. On seeing that sergeant Rowland was about to vacate the car for a second time, Fletcher waited until his man stood upright, then he wielded the spanner down with a force that could only be accomplished by a desperate man. He then slid smartly around the door which opened from front to back. As Sgt: Rowland sunk to his knees Cpl: Fletcher manoeuvred his way clear of the door and struck him twice more to be certain, then hustled the sergeant back inside arranging his body on the passenger seat. Having achieved this, he heaved the spanner into some nearby bushes, closed the car boot then jumped into the drivers' seat, reversed slightly, executed a complete turn and drove back to the bombed-out building they had passed earlier.

*

Having decided that Hornchurch aerodrome was now out of the equation, on account of old Danny Ross getting himself murdered in Stanley Road, DI. Selby reasoned that our RAF man would not want to stay around Hornchurch any longer than necessary, to which I fully agreed, simply because now we were thinking along the lines that if Danny Ross himself had been an enemy agent, whose job it had been to keep the police in Hornchurch running around like blue arse flies, then someone had dropped a serious bollock, because what they had actually achieved was to have this part of Essex running alive with half the bloody nations police force, which therefore meant that any enemy agent operating in this area would now be seriously hampered, not on account of the police force running around in turmoil, but now looking methodically for a murderer, who could well be connected with enemy agents.

Dave began to summarise "Now look Bill" he began "number one" he held up one finger "there's that RAF bloke who was enquiring about Old Ford Road, number two" a second finger went on display "our old girl opposite Bryant & May also claimed she'd clocked an RAF man 'angin' about the same night". Dave went silent a second or two, stared straight at me, a smile covering his face then added "and don't let's forget just recently that ticket collector at Hornchurch station reported a suspicious bloke in air force uniform". By now of course dear old Dave was looking real pleased with himself. I nodded my agreement to everything he had said. We then both took and lit a cigarette offered by our silent partner DC. Willis, who like always took one drag then blew a long stream of smoke from his nostrils. Dave offered up another two perfectly formed smoke rings, while I on the other hand took in a lungful of smoke and tried to speak at the same bloody time, which caused me to have a gigantic coughing spasm. Dave came to my rescue, giving me several pats on the back in an over-enthusiastic manner, nearly knocking me arse over tip. "Enough" I managed to croak. "Alright Bill?" he enquired. I just nodded while still gasping for breath. "Good" Dave acknowledged as a worried frown slipped from his face. "Now" he went on "one other thing I reckon worth mentioning, not long ago a railway worker reported some bugger had thrown a nut and bolt from a train, I think it was late last night. Anyway the bloody thing 'it' 'im on the leg, and now I'm awondering if that incident 'as anythin' to do with our boy" Dave ended his monologue there, shrugged his shoulders in a manner that indicated doubt.

It was at this point our silent partner spoke. He thoughtfully butted in with "I think Biggin Hill would be the likely place for him to be right now" DC. Willis solely advised. "Why Biggin Hill Tony?" Selby asked. "Well Sir, a few days ago they had trouble there. Apparently a jeep blew up and a couple of aircraft sustained some unexplained damage, and apparently no reason was established" Willis enlightened us. "He may be right there Dave" I threw in, then quickly added, "let's drive down and see". "Good idea. Willis get the bleedin' car," Dave ordered with authority, as though it was his bloody idea in the first place.

*

On arriving at the bombed-out building Cpl: Fletcher carefully arranged Sgt: Rowland's body under a heap of rubble, he then returned to what he now considered to be his car, settled himself behind the steering wheel, lit a cigarette and began taking stock of his situation. First off he realised it would be wise to quit Biggin Hill. However, there was a small matter of his personal belongings that must be considered, which were of course neatly stashed away in his bedside locker at Biggin Hill. He therefore decided this problem was his top priority and must be sorted. Next he would make his way back to Warlingham again and do some serious thinking.

Having then made up his mind, the bogus corporal executed an excellent three-point turn in his newly acquired Vauxhall car, and began to make his way to Biggin Hill airfield. The idea being to drive as close to the airfield that he considered to be reasonably safe, leave the car, cut across one of the adjoining fields, slip into his barrack room and relieve the locker of his personal belongings. After achieving this it would be straight back to car and on to Warlingham.

*

While breaking the speed limit, well on our way to Biggin Hill aerodrome, DI. Selby suddenly gave a few orders "Look Bill" he began turning towards me "when we get there you nip round back of the actual airfield, see if you can slip through a hedgerow of a neighbouring field somehow, then on into their living quarters, you never know you may surprise someone" Selby said all this as though we knew exactly what we were doing, which of course we didn't. "Never mind" I assured him "I'd be on me toes". He gave me a satisfied grin, then to DC. Willis added "And you Tony will stay with me" and that as they say 'was that'. Willis drove on in silence while Dave and I sat smoking on the back seat.

It must have been all of ten minutes later when we heard a siren starting to wail in the distance, and before the bloody thing fell silent two bloody bombs exploded in a field on our right, then a set of Pom Pom guns shattered the peaceful countryside with that distasteful pop-pop-pop, which had tormented us every bloody night since that great man warned us the battle of Britain must now begin. On reaching Biggin Hill, I did as Dave had commanded and slipped into a nearby field, then without any trouble at all worked my way onto the airfield itself. From there I made a spectacular dash for a row of huts I could see just off to my left. As I entered the first hut all hell broke loose, it appeared as though every gun they possessed on that poxy field opened fire at once, making an unbelievable racket. Even so, through it all I still heard two or three Stuka dive bombers come screaming down and release several sets of bombs. I naturally dived under a nearby bed for protection.

As it started to quieten down, the door through which I had entered suddenly flew open and banged shut, a voice screamed "Mein Gott". I rolled quickly from under the bed, came to my knees ready for action. 'Good, we've got our man' I thought, came off my knees swinging a vicious right hand and carried on swinging, that is until a bleeding train smashed straight into my face. Although it did nothing towards sweetening my disposition, it nevertheless somehow left me sharper, much quicker on my feet. So there I was ducking and weaving all round this sodden room, but then suddenly as the effects of that bloody train began to subside, I found myself jabbing at shadows and swinging at nothing more than bloody air.

19:

A CHANGE OF IDENTITY

Coming back to reality was a very weird experience, I could hear Dave saying "Calm down Bill, calm down" and yet another voice kept repeating over and over "Watch out there's a machine gun on our right". Then quite suddenly my head was clear. The voice worrying about the machine gun had obviously been mine. Dave's face came into focus, he sighed "Thank Christ for that" he mumbled as the worry drained from his face. "Thank Christ for what?" I rationally enquired. "You, yer silly sod" Dave answered with a smile and took an already lit cigarette from DC. Willis, claimed one drag for himself then passed it onto me. He next demanded, "What the bleedin' 'ell 'appened 'ere then?" So I began my story at the point where I'd negotiated my way through the hedgerow of an adjoining field.

*

After throwing a tin hat, which he'd scooped off someone's bed, into DS Augers face and seeing his adversary was now disorientated, the bogus Cpl: Fletcher moved swiftly to a large locker that stood beside a single bed, lifted a suitcase from under the bed and stuffed everything from locker into case, then smartly slipped out of the barrack room door, leaving DS Auger dancing around punching at shadows.

Back at the car which he had left a few hundred yards away from the airfield, he found that it was beginning to get dark. He therefore quickly opened the boot of the car, slung his suitcase inside, jumped in behind the wheel and began to make his way towards Warlingham. He realised of course that at some point he must dispense with the car and continue his journey on foot. Nevertheless he thought, it would be well worth it in the long run, just to spend a night in Sally, his landlady's bed. He'd known for a while that Sally had taken a liking to him, and therefore the next move was now up to him.

*

"Christ that means yer 'ad the bugger, why in 'eavens name didn't yer give us a bleedin' call for Christ sake?" Dave raved. "Coz I stepped in front of a bloody train, that's why me ol' mate," I defiantly replied while running my fingers over my face, trying to locate any damage I may have sustained. "Alright, any idea what the sod looked like?" Dave asked. "'Ain't gotta clue mate, can tell yer one thing though, he was big, at least six foot. I clouted 'im with one punch which caught 'im on the chest, where I thought his face should 'ave been" I cooed back at Dave with a faint smile.

*

After dumping his car in a small ditch behind a row of bushes near a place called Farleigh, Cpl: Fletcher had wiped all fingerprints from various parts of the vehicle, yet gave no thought to any other clue such as blood that may have stained the seats, in fact he had neglected many other unseen clues for that matter. Once again using his thumb he made his way back to Warlingham.

Entering the lodging house he purposely allowed the front door to bang shut behind him, just in case his landlady was entertaining someone. However now on seeing her glide gracefully down the stairs to greet him with that beautiful smiling face, it suddenly dawned on him just how desirable this woman really was, with a set of gleaming white teeth that seemed to flash through warm inviting well-shaped lips. A pair of deep blue eyes, all framed by a well-groomed hip length tangle of auburn hair, plus a slim well-rounded figure, with long shapely legs, which he somehow knew were going to be wrapped around him that very night.

On hearing the front door bang shut Sally, Cpl: Fletchers' landlady, knew at once the corporal was back. She took a quick look at herself in a mirror, tidied her hair, straightened her dress and began to make her way down to meet him. As she did so, she started to wonder if this tall attractive man would maybe for once respond to her feminine charms.

*

DI Dave Selby, DC Tony Willis along with myself DS Auger, all stood around the car smoking, I casually put forward my revelation "That's one thing Tony got right anyway" I informed DI Selby. "Yeah and what would that be Bill?" Selby enquired of me. "Well he did say Biggin 'ill is where our man would be, and he was bleedin' spot on there, wasn't he?" I replied. Dave looked from me to Tony "Yer know, yer bloody right at that, good work Tony" Dave said nodding to DC Willis. He then turned back to me with a half smile "and now I suppose we should ask our bright lad if he knows where next our man will be" Dave put forward with a touch of sarcasm, yet in a pleasant enough tone. "Who the bloody 'ell knows, perhaps he does, why don't yer ask 'im?" I invited. So Dave smiled and glanced at Willis "Well, any ideas son?" he mumbled. Tony returned Dave's smile, then with eyes settling on me replied "As a matter of fact I do" he then went silent. "Oh come on for Christ sake, don't keep us in bloody suspense son" Dave growled. I looked at Tony's face, there was a far away look in his eyes. "Yer know, I think that's bloody obvious Sir, yer see 'avin' now retired from the RAF as it were, which we can now assume on account of the bugger going to so much trouble to remove everythin' from his locker, now he'll be left with only one option, his lodgings, and that Sir is where we'll find 'im. The question now is, where the bloody 'ell's that?" came the final result of so much mental energy.

"Well that's bloody good thinkin' my ol' son, but if you can now just look a little deeper into yer crystal ball, perhaps yer can say exactly where we'll find 'is bleedin' lodgins'," Dave tried, adding more sarcasm. Nevertheless we were both surprised when DC Willis, the junior member of our team, offered us an even larger smile and astonishingly replied "Well, we know he won't go back to Hornchurch, he's obviously done what 'ad to be done there, and yer can count Bow out of the equation, coz he must know the police there are on to him by now so" DC Willis fell silent for a moment. "Yeah so?" Dave groaned impatiently "go on" he next tried encouragingly, but Willis stood staring off into space in deep contemplation, then suddenly he was back with us "Yes" he went on "the bugger will now keep well away from Biggin airfield itself, yet his lodgings won't be too far away. Let's find a bloody map somewhere" he concluded.

*

It had been a long passionate night for Sally, the bogus Cpl: Fletcher's landlady, it was a night Sally knew she wasn't likely to forget in a hurry. She realised there wouldn't be too many more nights like the one she'd just experienced, and that she thought was a pity because he had performed every erotic sexual act possible in bed that night, she'd found to her amazement, the whole experience had been most satisfyingly enjoyable, and now just thinking about it made her blush. However, he had revealed that night that he must exchange the RAF uniform for some civvies. He also added a change of name would be in order, he then announced 'my name will now be Reg. Martin' then he went on to explain that all the necessary documents required to prove he, 'Reg. Martin', existed were at that moment securely sewn into the lining of a large suitcase he'd retrieved from Biggin Hill. The next thing he had disclosed Sally simply did not want to hear 'I must consider a change of lodgings at some point' was his final remark.

*

Having spent some time searching around in the police car DI Selby finally stepped back with a book of maps in his hand. "'Ere we are Tony me lad" he chuckled handing it to DC Willis. Tony took map book, jumped behind the steering wheel, switched on a small light above his head, took pencil and pad from his pocket, and began searching each page until he found Biggin Hill. "Ah, 'ere we go" Tony sung out, and began running a finger around the Biggin Hill area. "Now let's see" he mumbled, then "right sir, I think we're more than likely find our man in a lodging house somewhere within a radius of five to ten miles from the Biggin airfield" Willis suddenly shrugged his shoulders "I don't know sir, there's lots of places he could be, the bugger could 'ave us runnin' around all bloody night" he moaned in frustration. Selby looking slightly crestfallen, tried encouraging our psychic junior partner. "Well never mind son just concentrate, yer know on places yer think the bugger might be" Selby put forward in a fatherly tone. "Ok, I'll do my best sir" Willis replied and slowly continued "Well look, there's the airfield" his finger stopped on Biggin Hill "there can yer see?" he added as Dave and yours truly leant further into the car. "Yeah right" Selby answered. "Well remember what I said?" DC Willis went on "five to ten miles, so that gives us Farleigh, Westerham and Warlingham" he stopped, sat pondering for a moment then continued "of course there's New Addington, maybe too far away though, or Keston, blimey could be anywhere in that area sir" Willis concluded, at the same time making a complete circle on the map with his pencil. "That's alright son, we'll try the bloody lot if needs be" Selby decided.

20:

MAN IN A BLUE SUIT

I've no idea why DI. Selby and I were called back to Bow Road police station, but from what I could gather from Dave, it would appear that the top brass were now considering whether or not they should call on MI5 for help in this case.

As Dave had related to me, at some point the Hornchurch police who were still investigating the murder in Stanley Road, Hornchurch, had somehow got wind of an RAF sergeant found dead in a bombed-out house near a place called Farleigh. It would appear that an autopsy had revealed that although the sergeants' body had been found buried under a pile of rubble, not one particle of dust had penetrated his lungs. There had also been some talk of a witness coming forward stating he had seen an RAF corporal getting in a car with the sergeant. When asked what type of car it was, the witness stated categorically it was a Vauxhall, which had been found some distance away. The coroner had also found several large bruises on the sergeants' head, so therefore concluded the sergeant had been killed somewhere else, and at this point would not rule out the possibility of foul play.

After having all this information laid on me, I nearly went stark raving mad. "In that bloody case, why the bloody 'ell did they bring us to this bleadin' dump?" I demanded in anger. "Well my ol' son, the 'super' thought it best to inform us that MI5 may now be taking the case over," Dave calmly reminded me, then further added, "anyway they still want us here for something or other"

We were now sitting at a table in a small room in the Bow Road police station. This room I dare-say, had been used for many things in the past, but at this particular moment served as a tea room. Dave offered me two saccharine for my tea. "One will do," I told him. "So now what the bloody 'ell we gonna do?" I asked Dave. He took a mouthful of tea, rubbed the back of his hand across his mouth, produced a pack of cigarettes selected one for himself, pushed what was left in the pack across the table towards me. As we lit up, a uniform constable came round and drew the big heavy blackout curtains, and not a moment too soon, for although it was getting dark already, none of us expected jerry to be over so early. Nevertheless here he was once again having another go at ruining our city and also doing his best to break that steadfast London spirit, with them bloody stuka dive bombers screaming down all over the bleeding place.

Dave and I being old infantry men from the first war, found we couldn't stay cooped up inside for too long. So like the best part of the Bow road police constabulary, we nipped out into the yard, where most mounted officers busied themselves trying to pacify frightened horses. "'Ere bugger this, too crowded 'ere Bill" Dave stated. "Yeah, let's move round front," I suggested. As we did so, three of them bloody stukas came screaming down releasing their poxy bombs with seemingly specific orders, which were to rid London of the two smartest detectives in England, but of course they missed. Dave and I had legged it, and by the time those bombs exploded, we'd almost reached Tom Thumbs arch, where we stood a minuscule amount of protection from the arch itself.

*

Having completed several alterations to a near new blue suit, which had long since been left behind in a wardrobe by a previous forgetful border of Sally's lodgings, she had presented it as a gift to her new lodger Mr: Reg. Martin, who had quite recently decided to change his name from Dick Fletcher. Reg. Martin slipped a wallet which contained several one-pound notes along with an identity card, into the inside pocket of his coat, handed a ration book to Sally, studied himself for a moment or two in the mirror. "Well, what do you think of your new lodger now Sally my girl?" he enquired. Sally stood arms folded while running a critical eye over him. "Now let me see, speaking as a woman, I would say 'what a very attractive man who has such style and charisma which seems to ooze from him'" she cooed softly slipping her arms around him and tilting her head slightly in order to receive his kiss on her full red beautifully shaped lips. After a while she pulled away from him gasping for breath. She kept him at bay with one hand on his chest. "My God" she panted. Reg. Martin smiled then took a step back "And as my new landlady?" he prodded. "As your new landlady" she repeated his words, "I would have taken one look at you in that blue suit and start to wonder how long it would take me to entice you into my bed" she replied then went into a fit of giggling, while Reg. Martin found it impossible to keep his hands off her as he manoeuvred this exciting woman onto a sofa in her front room.

*

Alright, so there we were stuck under Tom Thumbs bloody arch, and it didn't take long for us to realise Jerry was intent on keeping us there for a while. Roughly five minutes after our arrival, one of them bloody death on wheels 'pom pom' lorries stopped in the middle of an adjoining street, just a stones' throw away from our sanctuary. Dave shrugged his shoulders, nodded upwards as a steam train rattled its way over this fragile little bridge we were standing under, he also said something which I didn't hear owing to the noise of the train, then being deafened by bloody gunfire, bombs exploding, sodden air raid wardens running around screaming their bleeding heads off with 'Put that bloody light out' and of course, police cars flying about ringing their bloody bells, even coppers on foot blowing their lungs out on their whistles. Add to this those angels of the night; the white ambulances, tearing to newly bombed out buildings and rushing the injured to nearby hospitals with their bloody bells ringing and deafening everyone. In amongst all this fire engines chugging about with even bigger bells clanging away, of course usually by the time they'd arrived on the scene the place had burnt down anyway, all there was left to do was dig out the dead bodies and lay them out on the curb, and some bugger would still stay on the engine ringing that bloody bell.

Nevertheless with all this going on around us we both sat on the ground, lit a fresh cigarette each, while off in the distance we suddenly heard the delightful sound of an 'all clear'. Still, I daresay like me, Dave at that particular moment was back at Mons, or even on the Somme battlefield, and with me watching, as one friend after another was struck down. However apart from all those ambulances, fire engines and police cars still dodging about clanging their bloody bells, and of course don't let's forget the bloody racket of that 'all clear' siren which completed the overture, all was quiet, as far as the guns were concerned. Dave gave me a gift of two more smoke rings, then pinched out a half smoked cigarette. I tried returning his generosity, but once again near on choked me bleedin' self. "Never mind Bill let's nip back, see if our glamour boy driver Willis is still around" Dave suggested.

As it turned out, back at Bow police station we found DC Willis drinking tea and scoffing buttered toast. "Ah everythin' alright 'ere Tony?" DI Selby enquired while indicating to me he could do with another cigarette, which I duly supplied, 'naturally'. "Yeah, bit excitin' for a while there sir, but no one got hurt" he informed us through a mouthful of toast, then quickly held up his hand as Dave was about to speak "oh yeah" Willis went on "them buggers came all along the Mile End Road, machine guns blazin' away, you'll even be able to see where they hit that bleedin' bridge when it gets light" he stated with a distasteful look on his face, and pointed through a window next to where he was sitting. "Bridge, what bloody bridge?" I put in. "Cor blimey sarge: where the bleedin' 'ell you been?. This bridge across this bleedin' road" he told me, emphasising his point by pointing through the window again, towards Stratford bridge. "Oh that one," I offered back as though I'd been joking all along. Dave stepped in with "That means they 'ave torn up 'alf of bleedin' Stratford's High Street" he informed us, after which he gave me a quizzical look and two more perfectly shaped smoke rings. The smoke rings I chose to ignore. "Why the bloody 'ell would they machine gun that bridge, or the Stratford High Street for that matter?" Dave frowned.

*

Reg. Martin retrieved the small briefcase he'd left on top of the wardrobe in his room. Inside he carefully placed six hand grenades at the same time thinking how lucky he was to have such an obliging landlady. She not only offered her body for his manly needs, but also supplied him with the right kind of ordnance he required for any mission he may undertake. 'Yes I'm very lucky' he thought as he pushed six primers for said hand grenades into his jacket pocket. It was while sitting on his bed smoking, Martin started to contemplate just how he would go about distributing these few kind gifts, his landlady had supplied him with. She had however made one stipulation, which was to stay away from all petrol tankers, because many of the drivers in the past had done her several favours. Nevertheless he had already decided not to leave them out of the equation simply because they had probably slept with her. No, as far as he was concerned, they were all fair game.

21:

CARNAGE AT HEATHWAY

I don't know why I was so surprised to be on my way back to Hornchurch with DI Selby and DC Willis, after all we did have lodgings there. Still it came as a complete surprise when that phone in the Bow Road police station rang, and some bloody official from Scotland Yard told Dave Selby that until told otherwise he and his team would be working out of Essex, from Hornchurch police station to be precise. Dave cradled the phone, gave me a smile then said, "Right Bill, grab yer belongings because it's back to Hornchurch we go". So that was that.

All three of us travelled by train because DC Willis; our driver, had informed us the Bow Road constabulary could not spare a car for us, although this time it turned out alright, as we were travelling in daylight, and not one single bomb dropped anywhere near us for the one hour we spent on that bleedin' train. Anyhow when we finally arrived at Hornchurch, Dave made a point of speaking to several ticket collectors, until he'd finally netted the one who had been approached by the RAF corporal enquiring about the Hornchurch aerodrome. "Yers, he even gave me his name, Richard something I believe, hang on a minute I wrote it down, should be in here," the collector said as he sorted through a small desk that stood just inside a room that looked hardly large enough to accommodate the man, let alone a desk. Nevertheless he eventually gave Selby a name. "Yeah, here we are mate 'Dick Fletcher' that's what he'd said," the railway man told Dave. Dave thanked his informer and slipped back over to us. "There you are, at least we've gotta bloody name at last" Dave happily announced. "Yeah, well I wouldn't look so bleedin' pleased with yerself so soon, coz ol' Dickie boy 'as probably changed 'is 'andle and no doubt by now masquerading about as bleedin' Errol Flynn" I laughingly told poor old Dave, which I'm sure must have ruined any illusions he may have been harbouring about tracking this man down.

*

It was in fact the Fords and Briggs motor plants, these two main car factories in Dagenham, which were now working in conjunction with each other, turning out military vehicles for the British armed forces for the duration of the war, that Reg. Martin had decided would be his next target. Having by now grown a small beard that showed a touch of grey, as did his well-groomed head of hair now reposing under a neatly tilted trilby hat. Mr: Martin also found it to be appropriate to use a heavy strong wooden walking cane, and would constantly remind people how lucky he'd been getting away from Dunkirk with nothing more than just a leg wound.

Early that morning Sally had given her lodger Reg. Martin a thorough inspection. "Yes you'll pass" she stated, then quickly kissed him on the lips, closed the front door behind him, ran up stairs, flung herself on her bed and began weeping.

As before, Martin made his way back to London using his thumb. Once in London he boarded a train at Bromley-by-Bow bound for Dagenham in Essex.

*

As we'd done a couple of times previously the three of us took a nice stroll from Hornchurch rail station to the police station, and of course as before, we once again passed Stanley Road which this time appeared to be quite normal. Anyway, on crossing the road and approaching the police station, about a further five minutes walk, would you Adam and Eve it, that bloody air raid warning started, blasting our eardrums again, sodden thing. Still one thing we didn't have to worry about was them bloody guns on wheels contraption. Apparently Hornchurch didn't possess too many of those bleeding mobile greeting machines. So, all we had to contend with was some serious bombing and a bloody lot of anti-aircraft guns banging away. The racket of all this no doubt causing many a heart attack!

After Dave had spoken to some big wig by phone, DC Willis found himself travelling back to Elm Park in order to retrieve our car, while Dave and me started on a nice stroll down town back to our lodgings. However, whilst in town we decided to have a pint. We therefore stepped into the 'White Hart Hotel'. Because darkness was starting to creep in, we quickly manipulated our way through the heavy pub door, and smartly drew the blackout curtain hanging inside. Dave walked straight to the bar and ordered two pints of Old English ale, then very subtly informed the bar lady who we were, after which it didn't take him long to learn that an RAF corporal had indeed popped in for a pint, and very strangely had asked how he could catch a train to London, without the bother of walking to the Hornchurch station.

We continued our travel going by the Odeon cinema, on passed the 'Grey Towers' down towards Harrow Lodge park, we crossed the road heading towards our digs. It was then Dave gave me the benefit of some very shrewd brain work on his part. "Yer see Bill, that's something else we've learnt". "'Ave we?" I queried. "Look, this bleedin' RAF bloke is obviously operatin' from London" he handed me these few snippets just to keep me interested I'm sure, but then suddenly my brain started working. "'Ang about Dave, remember what Tony said, within a five to ten-mile radius from the aerodrome the bugger works from" I reminded Dave. "Right so that means the bugger must be beddin' down outside London" Dave slipped in. "Yeah, that's what Tony pointed out" I threw in. "Ok but most of those places Tony mentioned are way outside London anyway" Dave smugly remarked. "Well, as for that me ol' mate, think Tony was dead right when he said somewhere like Westerham, Farleigh or Warlingham, a place not too far from Biggin Hill itself" was my final comment. Dave was about to reply but instead, like myself, nearly jumped out of his bloody skin when two things happened. First, a big black Wolseley car drew silently alongside us, then started to blast away continuously on the bloody horn. The second thing that occurred was a stream of heavy bombs exploding in a back street close by, leaving Dave and me diving for the gutter with blood pressure dancing around in the heavens while we lay trying to stop the bloody ground shaking beneath us, meantime listening to red hot chunks of metal (they call this shrapnel) bouncing off the ground around us. Anyway when Dave and me jumped into the car, DC Tony Willis sped off and while doing so informed us Superintendent Jarvis would be expecting to see us at 8pm that evening.

Having arrived at our digs Dave announced 'a quick cupper wouldn't go amiss after that performance we've just experienced out there' and I thoroughly agreed.

Nevertheless I thought it rather strange, although we'd heard the air raid warning when we'd first arrived that day, nothing further untoward seemed to have disturbed this little village since, until suddenly from out of nowhere Jerry appeared, and had a bloody good go at eliminating me and Dave with some indiscriminate bombing. And of course don't let's forget our own bloody driver DC Willis who'd frightened the bleedin' life out of us with that poxy motor hooter. All this happened within a couple of seconds, not five minutes ago. So I'd say yeah a cuppa would go down a treat.

I was drinking my tea and studying a string of well-formed smoke rings DI Selby had just sent floating around the room, when he bestowed upon me his newly arrived at plan. "Look Bill," he began, "I expect the 'super' will be satisfied just seeing me tonight, so while lover boy Willis drives me back to the station, perhaps," and that's when I held up my hand indicating he should say no more "Yeah I know, perhaps I could rustle something up nice to eat, like a cooked dinner for a change" I finished his sermon with a smile, which he returned "there you are, right first time," he told me.

*

Reg. Martin departed the train at Heathway station, made his way along a rain drenched platform, climbed a set of stairs, handed over his ticket and walked out into one hell of a thunderstorm. However he could not help noticing the Heathway cinema which stood right opposite to where he was then standing. 'So' he thought, in order to while away an hour or two of daylight, it would be a good idea being entertained by John Wayne in his latest film called

'Stage Coach'. Martin strolled across the road, bought a pack of cigarettes at the cinema kiosk, paid for a ticket and was escorted through the darkness to a back row seat by a young lady carrying a torch. He settled back, lit a cigarette and began revelling in the pleasure of watching John Wayne shoot so many Red Indians. Ten minutes later a notice appeared on the screen stating that 'An air raid is now in progress' however Mr: Martin was enjoying the film so much, he therefore chose to ignore the warning, he was in fact quite content to stay watching the slaughter now running rife on the cinema screen.

Of course at that point Reg. Martin had no knowledge of the carnage raging outside, for all he knew Dagenham could have been obliterated outside, for in fact at that particular moment he was sitting in a building that had been built to last. No sound of anti-aircraft guns penetrated those walls and no exploding bombs were audible. It wasn't until sometime later a further message began winging its way across the screen announcing the 'All clear', as John Wayne bounded from one horse to another, that Mr: Martin gave any thought at all as to what was going on outside. It was none the less when a sudden blast from a rogue bomb exploded close to the back of that plush cinema, causing two heavy blackout curtain covered doors to swing wildly open leaving the curtains flapping inwards, that he thought it was time to leave.

*

The meal we finally got around to that night was not of my making. What I'd actually done in Dave Selby's absence, was to phone Florrie May my dear wife who was at our home in London. I asked her for suggestions and true to form dear old Flo immediately said 'what's wrong with fish and chips'. I sent two kisses down the line, gratefully thanked her and hung up, then took a brisk walk into that little Hornchurch village where I immediately found the local 'chippie'. I came away carrying two sixpenny pieces of cod and four penneth of chips. So that was the feast Dave and I sat down to that night. It was however whilst devouring this concoction, lavishly garnished with salt and vinegar, that my dear friend Dave endeavoured to narrate in his clumsy cockney way exactly what had transpired earlier between himself and the superintendent. "Look Bill I'll give it yer straight, like superintendent Jarvis 'anded it to me," he began. "Ok," I said while stuffing more chips into my mouth, at the same time Dave blew on a hot portion of fish before gingerly popping it into his mouth. "Yer see Bill, our forensic boys are not 'appy," he went on. "Yer don't say, why's that?" I asked. "Well it appears those two men recently found dead, or should I say 'murdered'". At that point he must have seen the doubtful frown on my face. "You know, one on that bomb site near Farleigh and that one 'ere in Hornchurch 'Stanley Road'" he jogged my memory. He then pushed away his plate and lit a cigarette (no smoke rings this time) which was just as well because it gave me a few minutes to digest what he was trying to explain. "Oh yeah I remember" I assured him. "Right so bear in mind two murders giving us two separate autopsies, one in Essex and one in London, and would yer believe, to quote Jarvis, 'both pathologists agree the modus operandi in both cases is the same, and that in turn gives us one perpetrator that committed these atrocities' which of course we now know is the RAF corporal. And there you 'ave it my ol' mate, that's as near damn it" Dave ended his sermon. "Are you sure about all that Dave?" I queried. He blew a smoke ring towards me, gave me a non-plus look and rattled off rather loudly "Course I'm bloody sure, ol' Jarvis even showed me the bloody report he received signed by two coroners and a Dr: Ronaldson, what else yer sodden need, yer silly bleeder". I glanced sternly at him "Who you calling a silly bleeder?" I challenged, and made to cuff him round the ear. He ducked back with a broad smile. "Alright yer grumpy bugger, was there any mention of them two brilliant detectives that was coshed?" I asked jokingly.

*

Stepping outside the cinema, Martin could see at once it was beginning to get dark. He studied the darkening sky for a moment, then stepped back inside through the blackout curtain into the semi dark of the foyer, located a nearby toilet. While inside the toilet Mr: Martin quickly transferred five grenades from his small case into his coat and trouser pockets, along with their primers. When entering the cinema he had noticed an alleyway which ran down the side of this particular cinema. He therefore decided to prime his last hand grenade so if possible he could lob this down said alley as a special thank you gift.

After delivering this grenade into an appropriate place alongside a few old dustbins, Martin nipped smartly across from cinema to Heathway station, paused, waited for the explosion to occur, which was taking longer than he'd expected. So while waiting decided to remove himself from the scene and in fact was about to enter a Woolworth store, when quite suddenly an explosion finally occurred coming from a direction diagonally opposite to where he then stood, and of course what followed was the inevitable chaos. Women screaming and all sorts of vehicles screeching to a sudden halt. Several shop windows breaking, and many police cars and fire engines arriving, people running in all directions. All this followed by an ambulance with bells ringing.

Reg. Martin could do no more than smile at the panic just one hand grenade could create. It was as he began to leave Heathway High Street and head towards Fords and Briggs factories, having already passed a small fire station, and was now cutting through a side street named Armsted Walk, that an authoritative voice behind him growled, "Oi you, hang on a minute". Reg. Martins blood ran cold, he turned ready to deliver a karate chop, but was relieved to see a middle-aged man wearing a tin hat with three letters adorning it 'ARP', offering him a walking stick "Ere mate you dropped this outside Woolly's" he was told. On accepting his walking cane he thanked and made to shake hands, but instead received a caution "Your gas-mask, where's your bloody gas-mask? You know it must be carried at all times" he was severely reprimanded. Martin lowered his head, slowly stroked his beard, looked slightly sheepish "Yes I am sorry about that, you see I lost it in that bombing which just occurred" he offered in defence, at the same time indicating back towards the cinema. "Oh well, nip along to the Town Hall, get a new one" he was advised.

22:

THE UNKNOWN SIDE TO PLUMPKIN

"For Christ sake Bill, give it a rest" DI Selby, my long-time friend implored me. "Give it a bleedin' rest, give it a bleedin' rest be buggered, just let me get my 'ands' on 'im, that's all," I retaliated.

This of course was part of a minor confrontation I'd had with DI Selby earlier that morning, then there had followed a brief spell of silence between us. After a while I'd realised how stupid it was, two grown men walking around the flat ignoring each other. I therefore decided enough was enough, and so with my irresistible smile glued to my face offered my old pal Dave a cigarette, said, "'Ere yer flat nose git, your turn to make the bloody tea ain't it?" He was sitting at the table, placed the cigarette in his mouth, was about to light it, but instead he leaned back then sprung forward with a lightening left hand jab which came straight towards my face. I parried this blow with my right hand, took a smart step back, well out of reach and yelled "Sorry, sorry you're not a git" to which he replied with satisfaction "That's better yer little squirt". "Yeah but you've got a flat nose anyway, and it's still your turn to make the bloody tea" I growled at him. Dave stood, walked over and studied his face in the mirror, turned to me with a grin and said "Yer know, yer bleedin' right Bill, I 'ave got a bit of a flat nose ain't I, never mind I'll make the tea" he chirped.

It was five minutes later when we heard our front door bell ring "Who in Gods' name is that?" Dave groaned. "Well it ain't me, I'm 'ere with you, ain't I?" was my quick reply. However within two minutes I'd opened the front door and in strolled dear ol' Plumpkin, our long lost pal from WW1 whom we all thought to be dead, but as we'd recently learnt had proved us all wrong. On entering he gave me a dig in the belly "Slow, always keep yer guard up Bill" he advised. "Right" I replied giving him a weird look as we went on through to the front room, where DI Selby sat having a quiet smoke and releasing several smoke rings which hung just below the ceiling before slowly fading away. As we were still engaged in drinking our tea, Plumpkin indicated he wouldn't be averse to a cuppa himself, so once again it was Dave on tea duty. After we'd exchanged pleasantries, Plumpkin got around to disclosing the reason for his visit. "Yer see sarge" he began, still addressing DI Selby as 'sergeant' which of course was Selby's rank in 1916 when we served together. Nevertheless at that stage neither Selby nor I bothered to correct him, instead we both smiled and Dave released another smoke ring.

In any event Plumpkin added "As you may 'ave guessed by now I'm with MI5" and that's when Selby raised his hand "'Ang on a minute 'ere, are you telling us, that tubby corporal we used to call Plumpkin is now a bleedin' MI5 agent? If so I don't believe it" Dave rattled off shaking his head. "Well it's bloody true" Plumpkin continued "and what's more I've been assigned to clear up this bleedin' Danny Ross murder case, that I believe you and young Billy 'ere made a right balls up of sergeant" Plumpkin stated with emphasis on the 'right balls up' part. Dave still couldn't accept it "No, you acting corporal Plumpkin, no mate I just don't believe it, MI5?" he further exclaimed. I also found this hard to swallow. "Well I'm sorry sarge but that's the way things are" Plumpkin firmly stated, then began chuckling. "Yeah, well let's 'ave less of the sergeant and more of either 'Sir' or 'Detective Inspector' from yer now on ol' mate" Dave raved at a then morose looking Plumpkin "and just for the record" Dave pointed at me "yer ol' mate Auger there is the sergeant now" Dave snapped. "Well yer maybe DI Selby now me ol' mate, but you'll always be that 'RB' Sgt: Selby we first met sitting in that dugout on the Somme battlefield in June 1916, so there!" Plumpkin remonstrated defiantly. Nevertheless Selby scratched his head, looked towards me and mumbled "'Im, MI5?" Plumpkin nodded his head and said "Listen"

*

By the time he'd arrived at Fords Motor Company, Martin was undecided as to where he should deliver his remaining five grenades. However on thinking back to that solitary grenade he'd deposited alongside Heathway cinema, Reg. Martin came to the conclusion that he'd armed it with one of Germany's new type of time delayed action primer. So therefore Sally, his landlady, must have inadvertently placed the wrong detonators with these grenades. None the less it now occurred to him this could in fact lead to his advantage, in as much as it would lengthen the period of time he had to vacate any area he chose to deposit one of these death-dealing contraptions.

Reg. Martin spent roughly half an hour reconnoitring Fords factory. On reflection decided just getting through the gate would present an unnecessary problem in itself, he therefore concluded Fords should be avoided completely and in preference concentrate on Briggs Motor Bodies, it was therefore to this end that Martin settled on exploring a part of Briggs known as the River Plant. He at once realised this part of the factory was decidedly easier to enter than Fords had been. He strolled casually through an open gate and on into what appeared to be a dining hall, no doubt for the workers, he thought. Martin then moved further on and slipped through another unlocked door, where he discovered a row of musical instruments, consisting of bagpipes and drums. He concluded this was also for the workers, a recreation room no doubt obviously used by the firms' band. It was however a constant humming coupled with the continuous individual revving of engines, that attracted him to a window which was slightly higher than usual, cut into an internal wall. Nevertheless he found by standing on a chair that stood just under the window, he was allowed to view a complete assembly line of Bren gun carriers seemingly in the final stages of completion. On studying this spectacle further, he noticed that as each vehicle reached the front of said assembly line it was then shunted to one side, in order to be replaced by another.

*

Plumpkin went on to explain just how he'd managed to convince the authorities that he was well suited to become a member of the MI5 fraternity. Nevertheless Dave Selby and I found it extremely hard to believe dear old Plumpkin was a 'secret squirrel', even though he went out of his way to explain how on being demobbed in 1919, he'd spent two years studying and had subsequently passed all relevant exams. After this another year of studying had followed, and then he was put into a training programme which went on for another two more years. At the end of this he was finally accepted on a temporary basis for a trial period, until he'd proved himself as a qualified field operative.

Even so, Selby still had reservations and insisted on the last word. "Well I can only congratulate yer Jeff on yer achievement, but to me you'll always be that dozy 'Acting Corporal Plumpkin' from '2' Platoon 1st KRRs" Dave chuckled. "Well I wouldn't 'ave it any other way mate" Plumpkin retorted as he handed round a pack of cigarettes, then a period of silence followed. I could see Plumpkin studying both Selby and me as he sat puffing hard on his cigarette, then suddenly our old mates face creased into a wide grin and as his eyes went to each of us in turn, he recited the following; "'Yer know I still can't believe I'm sat 'ere with my two ol' pals, Billy Auger, the barrow boy, our platoon marksman and finally company sniper, and his bleedin' mentor Sgt: Selby, the battalions favourite Sergeant. The very two men I went over the top with in that butchers field, the bleedin' Somme, all them years ago". Needless to say by the time Plumpkin had quit reminiscing, all three of us were well and truly choked up with emotion. I even found myself mopping a tear from the corner of my eye.

However, in the middle of this nostalgic scene DI Selby found cause to rush out and open our front door. To his amazement he discovered DC Willis, hammering madly on the door. Plumpkin and I looked at each other in puzzlement, then we heard Selby bark "Alright son why all this bloody excitement, where's the bloody fire for Christ sake?" Suddenly the room door where Plumpkin and I sat burst open and both men entered with Selby still persevering "alright, alright calm down son" he tried, showing a touch more patience. I offered Willis my half-smoked cigarette, after one gigantic puff it was back with me. "Now lad just sit quietly and tell us what's 'appened," Selby said in a fatherly tone.

*

Martin quickly observed the putty holding the observation window in place was still slightly damp, and could therefore easily be removed. He first made sure the door through which he'd entered, was closed. He then scraped a good deal of putty from around said window, making sure to leave just enough to hold the glass in place for the time being. After this exercise he carefully armed his five remaining grenades, placed three of them near to hand, replaced the remaining two in his jacket pocket. Next he silently removed the glass and lowered it carefully, after which he took two grenades, pulled the pin from each of them, released their safety levers and in an underarm fashion, tossed both missiles through a now clear space. Both grenades ended their journey alongside the conveyer belt. He quickly repeated the process with his third grenade, which rebounded off a leading carrier straight into a vehicle that had already been shunted to one side. He then very swiftly gathered together his walking stick, hat and small case, studied his surroundings for a moment, decided to leave it undisturbed and left.

*

"Are yer tellin' us that some bugger 'as tried blowin' up the 'Eathway cinema?" DI Selby barked. "Well from what I can make out that's about the size of it sir" DC Willis confirmed excitedly. "What, in broad bleedin' daylight?" I broke in with. "Yeah that's what I'm sayin', and if we jump in the bleedin' car now, we could be there in half-hour, and what's more they reckon a couple of people saw this bleeder chuck some sort of explosive down an alley, and then just walk calmly away sir" Willis rattled off in that bloody machine gun like fashion, the way youngsters are inclined to speak these days. "Right, well don't 'ang about, come on let's go" Selby commanded. "Ok Dave I'll be comin' with yer, and remember this, I'm MI5 which means yer do like I say, alright!" Plumpkin made his position abundantly clear.

*

It wasn't until he, Martin, had slipped out of the Briggs River Plant gate and was halfway across the road heading towards Dagenham's Telephone Cables Ltd factory, which stood almost opposite, that he heard three muffled explosions. A knowing smile caressed his face as he hurried on. Now approaching the TCL factory, he thought at first he might have to negotiate his way over a heavy gate into the factory yard. However he was pleasantly surprised, it was already open. So with no other obstacles encroaching his progress, Martin simply walked straight through the gate and into a small office which proudly displayed 'Personnel' on the door, where he found a young lady seated behind a rather large desk. On seeing Reg. Martin enter she stood to greet him with a well practised smile, then pulling a wool cardigan comfortably around her shoulders said "Oh I'm sorry love, you're too late, all personnel staff have left. If you can come back tomorrow about 10am, you might be lucky, because we're taking on more cable joiner assistants" she happily told him, on the assumption he was looking for employment. She then retrieved a bunch of keys from a desk drawer, removed a jacket from the back of her chair and stood to one side, waiting for him to leave. Being taken slightly aback by her reaction he nodded, thanked her for her trouble and moved as though about to leave, but instead as she leant forward to insert the key in the lock, he moved swiftly round her and delivered two vicious lightening-like karate chops, one each side of her neck. He quickly slipped an arm around her, preventing her from falling and banging against the door. After lowering her dead body to the ground, he stepped further back into the room, took both remaining grenades from his pocket, pulled out both pins, but still held both levers in place. He then walked over and opened an adjoining door that he assumed would lead straight into the factory itself, it was the sound of machinery that led him to believe this. He then released each lever in turn thus arming the two remaining missiles, he then rolled the penultimate grenade through this now open door, firmly closed it, and without hesitation placed the last grenade on his latest young victims desk. He then moved swiftly to the door of his original entrance, stepping over the young lady's body as he went, made a quick exit and smiled to himself as two explosions occurred behind him. He began retracing his steps heading towards the Grange cinema, which in turn would lead him onto Heathway railway station.

23:

A BEARDED MAN OF DISTINCTION

As it turned out we arrived at Heathway station twenty minutes after leaving Hornchurch. Plumpkin immediately pushed his credentials under a police officers' nose who'd been left on guard duty. He was then permitted to pass down to where some sort of devise had obviously exploded. Of course DI Selby and his faithful Sergeant Auger were also in attendance, having left DC Willis with our car. To start with Plumpkin began asking this friendly constable, who had taken it upon himself to escort us to this wretched scene, where we could clearly see a small crater coupled with one or two perforated dustbins lying about, "Now PC Hill" Plumpkin began "exactly what can you tell us about this little 'argy bargy'?" "Well, what the forensic boys say, 'some devious bastard must have lobbed a bloody grenade down this alley, then quickly pissed off'" PC Hill explained with practiced eloquence. "Oh I see, and that's all yer can tell us?" Plumpkin probed. It was now obvious Plumpkin had run out of questions. That's when DI Selby stepped in. "Look Officer Hill can you tell us, did anyone witness this happening?" he immediately asked. "Ah, funny you should ask that sir" PC Hill replied while lifting his helmet, mopping his brow with a clean handkerchief, after which transferring his attention to the inside of his helmet. "Yes man, go on" Selby urged. "Well sir, we've had several members of the public come forward stating they saw an old fellow sporting a beard and a heavy walking cane. Apparently he simply walked out of

Heathway cinema and lobbed something down the bleeding alley" PC Hill stopped there and along with his three superiors lit a cigarette. Just to make my presence felt, I intervened with "So that's all the information you can give then constable?" He looked at me as though I'd been thrown into the pot at some expense, as just another inconvenience he must endure.

Quite suddenly another thought seemed to float into officer Hills mind. "Of course all of the witnesses stated this old codger had long gone before any bloody explosion occurred" he rapidly expressed. Now it was Selby's turn "Anyone hurt you know of?" Officer Hill now handed Selby the treatment he'd bestowed upon me, staring at Dave as though he should have known no-one was injured. "Well?" Selby persisted, showing signs of impatience. "No, not to my knowledge sir" came a short reply from PC Hill whilst shaking his head and replacing his helmet.

Plumpkin stepped in "Ok officer, keep up the good work" he said, glancing towards me with that same look in his eyes I'd first seen in 1916, when he'd decided to tag along with me charging across that bloody Somme killing field. "Look, I don't know about yous two, but I'm fresh out of fags" Plumpkin stated on patting his coat pockets. "Ok, well follow me" I invited, and started across the road to the tobacconist which at that time stood alongside Heathway station. "There you are cock, in there" I pointed. However as Jeff made to walk through an already open shop door, he almost bumped into some old boy, who at that moment was in the process of blowing his nose with an extra large handkerchief which covered best part of the old codger's face. Nevertheless Jeff moved nimbly around this old feller and with a smile apologised for his clumsiness in nearly flattening the poor old sod. In return he received a grunt of annoyance, but then needless to say, we entered into a flash back moment of a dear old Plumpkin we'd known in yesteryear, as he performed a fairy tread-light neat fantastic step around the old boy, caught his foot in the blokes heavy cane, and as we'd seen so many times before, went arse over tip, ending his excursion in an untidy heap cuddling the heavy walking cane. Of course Selby and myself being chief witnesses to this fiasco were, as you can imagine, creased over with laughter. Still regardless of Plumpkin's predicament, his playmate quickly snatched up his cane and left the shop, pocketing his handkerchief as he went. This in turn offered us an unrestricted view of the mans' face, which at once revealed a proud possessor of a neatly trimmed moustache and a beautifully shaped beard to match, which prompted DI Selby to remark "there me ol' cock goes a man of distinction" and me, silly bugger Auger, thoroughly agreed "Yeah, the gents certainly got class alright". I concurred. Then as in bygone days we set about lifting this brilliant MI5 agent Plumpkin, from an uncomfortable tangled position alongside a glass counter, to his feet.

*

Reg. Martin had hastened to retrieve his walking stick and quickly leave the tobacconist, violently cursing himself for getting tangled up with some idiot who had eventually tripped over Martins walking stick and gone sprawling into the shop counter, thus ending this unfortunate encounter. However it wasn't just the ungainly antics this stupid man had performed, while his two companions stood by laughing, that had aroused his awareness, no what had caused this was that he had recognised the blonde-headed man who'd accompanied this clown, thereby catching him completely off guard. And although it wasn't entirely his fault, Martin nevertheless considered it to be very remiss of him for allowing the situation to escalate in such a way. Yet after giving the matter some serious thought, he realised it would be highly unlikely for this blonde fellow to recognise him as the adversary he had encountered at Biggin Hill airfield when they first met, simply because he, Martin, had instantly smashed a tin hat into the blonde fellows face, and left him there throwing punches at nothing. Plus the fact, that since that first encounter, he Martin, now sported a growth of facial hair, which he had recently cultivated in order to change his appearance.

In any case Martin decided to vacate the scene altogether, and to this end stepped into Heathway railway station, where to his amazement he discovered two burly policemen checking each would-be passenger, as they first purchased a ticket then made their way towards the platform. He quickly pulled back out of sight, then slowly eased himself outside where he mingled with a substantial group of inquisitive diehards, who'd accumulated on the scene after the bomb exploded some time ago. Martin lingered while composing himself and contemplating his next move. After several minutes spent watching police cars, fire engines and the odd ambulance dodging here and there, he suddenly decided to brazen it out, reasoning that under the circumstances this, no doubt, would be his best option. He therefore entered Heathway station with a determined stride and confidently made to address the constable standing by the ticket office. However, Martin was slightly taken aback when the constable raised his hand before any words were exchanged, "Excuse me sir, you do realise you're not carrying a gasmask," he was again solemnly reminded. This meant Martin had to think fast 'bugger it, bloody gas mask again' he cursed inwardly, nevertheless regardless of the police officers obvious suspicion Martin went ahead and confidently purchased a ticket to Barking. Turning back to by now a very suspicious policeman he explained how he'd been in the cinema when the explosion had occurred, and everyone had been advised to leave as quickly as possible and in his haste he'd simply neglected to retrieve his gasmask, which he was sure would still be where he'd left it. Martin also humbly thanked the constable for his concern and assured him he would nip straight over and claim the gasmask forthwith.

On entering a somewhat damaged cinema foyer, Martin made a snap decision by asking a dishevelled usherette if anyone had come across a lost gas mask. "Oh darling, you're in luck, there's three of those bloody contraptions hanging on that door over there" she pointed. Martin made an exaggerated show of selecting the right apparatus, just for the girls benefit, thanked her and left. Back at Heathway railway station he strolled straight past a now far more relaxed policeman, while holding a little brown cardboard gas mask box on high, and pleasantly indicating to the officer he'd found it, then quickly disappeared down the steps onto the platform.

24:

WHERE DID HE GO?

We'd left DC Willis sitting in the car opposite Heathway Station sometime earlier, although we'd found out later when he picked us up, that he'd been ordered away from the scene. Having driven the bloody thing halfway around the houses, ending up in a place called Rugby Road, Becontree, which was some distance away. And all this in order to be well clear of the danger zone where a bomb had exploded some time ago at Heathway cinema. However on returning to us and now pulling away from outside the tobacconist, Willis turned to DI Selby with raised eyebrows, at the same time nodding to Plumpkin and me who were then lounging on the back seat. "I suppose you'll all wanna visit Briggs Motors and that Cables place now?" he enquired offhand. Plumpkin and Selby both looked stunned, but Selby got in first with "Why?" "Oh blimey sir, ain't you 'eard, both places 'ave been bleedin' nobbled, and some wicked bastards murdered a young office bird, some sort of receptionist I think, anyway on top of that the cheeky bleeder chucked a couple of bleedin' bombs around in Briggs and a couple more in that Cables place" Willis rattled off. There followed a stunned silence "Jesus Christ why the bloody 'ell wasn't we informed sooner?" Selby stormed in pure frustration. "Well I don't know sir, I only just 'eard it me bleedin' self, 'twas on the radio as I was coming to pick you up" Willis came back with his brilliant defence. "Well, when the bleeden' 'ell did all this 'appen?" Selby then wanted to know. "I'm not sure, must 'ave been late last night or a little while ago, any case was after Heathway cinema copped one sir" Willis informed us. "Can't 'ave been last night, we'd 'ave 'eard about it before now" Plumpkin broke in.

"Well whatever, I'll drive yer straight to Briggs River Plant, it's where it all began, so they say" Willis hyped up for effect. After a minute or two, DI Dave Selby turned to me "Look Bill, when we get there, you and glamour boy 'ere" he nodded at Willis 'ave a word with one or two of the locals, they invariably know something that would take us a couple of bloody weeks to discover" he explained to me. I in turn gave him a half grin "Ok Dave" I said, knowing exactly what he inferred. You see, some time ago, Dave and I had discussed this problem of police investigating a crime. We'd both agreed that in most cases where a crime's committed, it's the people living in that particular area who will invariably, if asked the right questions, ultimately point the investigating team in the right direction. Which of course can be confirmed by our old Ford Road incident, where the old lady who thought she was being gassed, put us onto an RAF man creeping about at night, and this quick-witted clever little DS, yours truly, could have grabbed that bugger a few days later had it not been for a miscellaneous tin helmet. In any event by the time Willis anchored our car outside Briggs River Plant, a small crowd was in evidence, so for the benefit of this crowd, DI Selby and Plumpkin put on a supreme show of confidence when entering the River Plant gate. As for me, I latched on to Willis and quickly briefed him on what sort of person we were after netting "You know, the ones who can't stop talking" I told him. "I've gotcha Bill" he replied. So we began our quest to wheedle out one or two of the most promising individuals.

Sometime later, DI Selby pushed his way through a somewhat riotous crowd, cottoned onto me, saying "'Ere Bill, would yer believe, whoever it was apparently lobbed a couple of bloody grenades through a small window, completely destroying two Bren gun carriers and rendering a conveyor belt practically useless in the bargain". Dave passed this information over as though the war would be lost because of it. I gave him a casual look and for the want of something better to say simply muttered "Christ" and left it at that. Suddenly Plumpkin materialised "Blimey Bill, some bugger caused a bit of bleedin' chaos in there" he informed me, while indicating with his thumb back where he'd come from, and thereafter taking and lighting a cigarette I'd offered him.

*

Martin alighted from the train at Barking station, then booked a further ticket to London, where he had eventually been able to arrange a lift back to Warlingham. He'd already decided to keep away from his place of lodgings for the time being. So to this end found for himself a local park bench where he could have a quiet smoke and relax awhile.

However, it was whilst smoking he reprimanded himself concerning a couple of factories he'd overlooked when in Dagenham, for instance 'Ever Ready Batteries' and 'May & Baker chemical factory'. Was at that moment Martin promised himself he would make a special trip back to Dagenham in order to rectify this mistake. In the meantime, he realised by now the Military Police along with Special Branch no doubt, would be searching for him along with that British over rated MI5 bunch. He therefore had a quick change of mind, and now considered the sanctuary of his lodgings would offer him a far better degree of safety, and hopefully would also afford him a pleasant evening in Sally's bed.

Reg. Martin entered his lodgings with trepidation, listening for any unusual sound, while slipping his front door key safely back in his coat pocket. This time he refrained from calling his landlady's name, mainly because the house seemed so quiet and unwelcoming. Regardless of this he began to wonder, could Sally already be entertaining someone, and with this thought in mind, he shuffled silently down the hallway and began to ascend a narrow staircase. However on reaching the top step, Martin became aware of a light shining through a gap at the bottom of Sally's bedroom door. He cautiously moved forward, silently opened her door and was amazed to see Sally sitting in bed brushing her hair with the top half of her body completely naked. He also noticed two American air force uniforms carelessly thrown over two chairs. At this point a pang of jealousy overcame him, nevertheless by this time Sally had seen him and was frantically motioning for him to leave. He looked at her with a frown, then nodding at the uniforms raised two fingers whilst mouthing the word 'two'? She answered with a swift nod of her head and another desperate plea for him to leave. She also indicated by pointing, that they were both in the bathroom next door and wouldn't be long. Martin very softly closed Sally's bedroom door, after which he made his way along this dismal upstairs landing to a spare room at the far end. He knew Sally always kept this room locked, nevertheless he also knew where she kept the key, which was in fact, in full view, reposing on a small tea trolley which stood on this dim landing.

Ronald Cove

*

It was when DI Selby and Plumpkin rejoined DC Willis and me in the car, that we learned from Selby, how some silly bugger had removed the body of the young office girl who'd been murdered earlier, in the Cable factory in Dagenham. "Where'd they take the poor cow?" I asked. "Fucked if I know" came a crisp reply with a hint of frustration, as they each in turn slammed shut their respective back car doors. "So now what?" I tentatively enquired. "I'm buggered if I know, the whole things a bloody cockup, there's that lot over there" Selby nodded towards Briggs Motor Plant "no bloody night guards" he went on "now this bloody lot let some silly sod of a Doctor order an ambulance to take the dead girls' body to the bleedin' 'ospital, makes yer wonder what the bloody 'ell's next" Selby stormed. At this point, I hesitated a moment wondering whether or not I should add a touch more joy to poor old Dave Selby's joyous day. However I knew he'd eventually have to hear about another balls up we'd made between us. I first paved the way by passing him a cigarette, then softly said, "I don't suppose yer wanna 'ear what someone told our lady's man 'ere then?" Dear old Dave gave me a discerning look while our lady's man Willis, at that time seated by my side, elbowed me in the ribs and muttered, "For Christ sake Bill". Dave leant forward "go on Bill, let's 'ave it then" he sighed. Plumpkin also suggested I shouldn't take my secret to the grave. I therefore reluctantly, roughly repeated what Willis had told me after mingling with the crowd earlier. "Well, it's like this" I began, gently trying to soften the blow. "Oh for Christ sake get on with it Bill" Selby exploded. "Alright, alright" I yelled back "Now like I was saying, some bloke told Tony he'd seen this feller with a beard carrying a heavy bloody walking stick, this bloke said 'he'd come out of Briggs River Plant just before them two bloody bombs exploded'. Now I reckon that's the same bearded warrior Plumpkin tangled with in that bloody tobacconist". Here, I decided they'd 'ad enough good news for one day, so was prepared to leave it there, but, when no one else spoke I quickly added, "Well, what d'yer reckon?" I'd hardly got the words out when "What the bloody 'ell do I reckon?" Selby began, and then went into a long session of polluting the air with a long drawn out string of foul mouth blaspheming.

25:

A DISCOVERY

After entering a rather small dingy room, Martin searched around for a light switch and quickly discovered it didn't make too much difference to this dismal looking room anyway. He then checked the blackout blind was in place, which somehow he knew would be, thereby keeping this room in permanent darkness day and night. He moved across the tiny room to a double door wardrobe standing against the wall opposite the door. He casually opened both doors and gazed in amazement on finding himself confronted with a cupboard full of military weapons. He considered it to be enough to supply a small army. Having discovered all these goodies made him rush over and immediately lock the room door, which he had carelessly neglected to do when entering. However it wasn't until Martin got back to sorting through this incredible find, that he began to realise the significance of such an enormous amount of ordnance in a private dwelling. Having closed both wardrobe doors, Martin noticed a suitcase resting on top of said wardrobe. In the event however, decided to leave it for the time being, then glancing around this small dingy room, discovered several similar, if slightly smaller cupboards, where he went on to reveal even more killing devices. It suddenly became quite clear to him that Sally had obviously been ingratiated into this country, before hostilities occurred, and had laid dormant, then moved into the realm of sleeping agent and of course meanwhile had received regular supplies of weaponry. Once hostilities began her roll had changed and she became a friendly landlady, whose clientele would consist of enemy agents to whom she would be in a position to supply with any necessary ordnance they may require.

Meantime it would seem, that Sally being a very attractive woman, wasn't adverse to satisfying her sexual needs by entertaining a few of the local military boys in her bed at night. Whether or not she did this for self-satisfaction or indeed in order to ascertain any information they may inadvertently pass on, Martin had no way of knowing.

*

By the time us four avenging angels arrived back at our digs in Hornchurch, we were in a right kerfuffle, well that's to say three of us were. As for DI Selby there's not a lot I can say really, only that he was in an uncontrollable rage, still raving on about how some bloody Doctor could take it upon himself to have a body removed from a crime scene before we got there. "It's bloody diabolical what these silly bastards do these bleedin' days" Selby growled. Naturally both Plumpkin and I stayed well out of his way, knowing from old that Dave Selby could be a bloody hard man to handle when in one of these moods. However, DC Willis eventually took the bull by the 'do dahs' so to speak. "Look sir, all the cursing in the bleedin' world won't put things right" Willis boldly pointed out. Suddenly all went quiet, Selby's mouth clamped shut, his eyes first took in Plumpkin's solemn face, then swung round to me. I gave him a non- committal smile, then Dave's eyes settled on Willis, and in a flash all the tension disappeared, then Dave Selby said in a controlled voice "You're bleedin' right son,

I was getting' carried away with meself for a minute there, sorry about that lads," he apologised. Some five seconds elapsed before he added, "I noticed neither of my two brave friends step forward to shut me up though". After which he accepted an offered cigarette from Willis and once again commenced releasing several smoke rings around the room. Both Plumpkin and myself revelled in complete silence.

It was now Plumpkin's turn to act as 'Mother', so he first wired in setting the table, next making and serving tea all round, followed by a couple of slices of thinly buttered toast each. Now with us all seated at the table DI Dave Selby started enlightening us on just how many 'cock-ups' we'd made so far. "Right" he began "for a kick off we're all invited to first take a very pleasant ride all the way over to Dagenham's Heathway cinema, where this charming bloke's chucked somethin' down an alley alongside this bleedin' picture 'ouse, which we've been told exploded several minutes later. Now, when asked to describe the perpetrator, they tell us he was about five feet ten inches, 'ad a well-groomed beard and carried a heavy walking stick, ring any bells so far?" Dave broke off there, downed a mouthful of tea then assassinated half a slice of toast, while we three waited in anticipation. "Now where was I? oh yeah, next Plumpkin 'ere, who I might add should 'ave been in charge of this bleedin' entourage from the start, never mind, he goes waltzing into this bleedin' tobacconist without any 'elp from us bleedin' lot, does a light fantastic with some bleedin' warrior who is also a proud owner of a heavy walking stick and would yer believe, also has a beard" at this point Dave gave a despairing shake of his head, then executed the second half of his toast before continuing, "ok, next what 'appens, we all go for a quiet evenings drive to that bloody factory, Briggs Motor

Bodies, where some buggers now making a fortune producing of all things, Bren Gun carriers, but low and behold 'ere again, what do we find? Some buggers preceded us and he's been kind enough to deliver two bleedin' bombs onto the River Plants' assembly line. Then apparently he'd nipped 'appily across the road, murdered a young defenceless office girl, on top of which he also left them a couple of goodies that exploded sometime after he'd pissed off" Here a sudden gap appeared in Dave's narrative while he lit a fresh cigarette. The rest of us waited in vain for the inevitable smoke ring, instead a stream of smoke was followed by "and 'ere of course we all know it took three top-class Scotland Yard detectives and a brilliant MI5 agent to discover this man also sported a well-trimmed beard and need I say, carried a heavy walking stick". Here Dave's narrative came to an abrupt end. Three smoke rings then began a journey towards the ceiling. After all this well earned verbal abuse Dave had subjected us to, I looked round at the other two faces, and could quite understand the despondent looks I received in return. Nevertheless Selby hadn't quite finished "Well come on yer bunch of bloody 'alf wits, where d'yer reckon we go from 'ere?" he invited. As it turned out none of us could think of a bloody thing to say, so we maintained a continuous silence while puffing hard on our cigarettes, that is until our brave glamour boy Willis stepped in with "What I wanna know is where the bleedin' 'ell this clown came from in the first place?" At which point his face screwed up and his hands parted in an obvious attempt to express himself. I was about to explain but Selby jumped in first. "Where in Gods' name yer been son? I thought it was common knowledge by now, this bearded sod is one of them brave bleeders the German high command decided to throw in amongst our boys at Dunkirk. Of course they 'ad to take their chances on the beach, but those buggers that got through could play havoc in this country whenever they like, and I daresay the bleedin' country's flooded with the buggers now" Dave patiently explained. "Yer know I've been thinkin' Dave" Plumpkin butted in, only to be cut short with "I do 'ope it's somethin' sensible this time Jeff" Dave croaked despairingly. "Well, I was thinkin' 'ow about another cup of tea?" "Oh for Christ sake, I ought 'ave known, yer bleedin' idiot" Dave laughed. And whilst we were all taking the 'Michael' out of Plumpkin, it suddenly occurred to me what I would do in the bearded warriors place.

*

After hearing the front door downstairs close, Reg. Martin came out of his landlady's spare room where he'd discovered the substantial hoard of killing devices. Having made sure to lock the door and replace the key on the trolley where he'd found it, he then moved silently along to Sally's bedroom door, where he stood listening for a moment. When no sound was forthcoming, Martin quickly but silently entered her room and to his amazement found Sally lying stretched out naked on the bed. She turned her head towards him "Ah, I wondered when you'd be along" she said invitingly while patting the bed beside her, thereby implying he should join her. A surprising look slid onto Martins' face. Sally couldn't help but laugh. "But you've just 'er' with those two" he mumbled while nodding back through the door. "So, who's counting?" Sally defiantly countered. Martin then knew no matter what, he couldn't refuse this blatant offer and quietly closed the door behind him.

As Martin slowly undressed, a far off air raid siren began wailing, nevertheless this did not distract him from his task that now lay before him. Later while sitting together in bed smoking, Martin engaged Sally in a long question and answer session, concerning all the bits and pieces he'd discovered in that dingy spare room along the landing, before he'd walked into her bedroom and got lucky.

26:

A ROOM GOES MISSING

Anti-aircraft guns were continuously coughing high explosive shells skywards at a group of persistent Dornier bombers as they constantly pressed home their attack on Hornchurch aerodrome, while three brave ex-soldiers, now detectives, stood in the dark outside our rented flat's front door, making idiotic comments about how we'd have handled this situation in the last war. Plumpkin voted for a six-man squad of rapid firing riflemen, to engage this well out of range enemy. Where as I on the other hand, favoured one man with a German modern Mauser sniper's rifle. "Yep, that should do it" I said confidently. It was however Dave Selby, who once again pointed out the errors of our ways. "Yer pair of bleedin' dummies, don't yer know things 'ave changed since the first lot? First off, them bloody things fly well out of rifle range, and what's more them buggers would laugh at our feeble attempts to ground them" Dave cut our hopes down with these few chosen words of wisdom. "Yeah, you're bloody right Dave" I admitted. Plumpkin stubborn as ever wouldn't agree. "Well I don't know Dave, half a dozen good riflemen, who could say" he persisted. "Yeah right mate, they're flying at twenty thousand feet, good on yer" Dave capitulated, at the same time giving me a nod and whispering "'he's fuckin' nuts.'" "When d'yer find that out?" I replied. As the gun fire eased off slightly, DC Willis rejoined us. "Is that young lady alright Tony?" Selby asked referring to Willis's landlady who he'd popped in to see was ok. "Oh yeah, she is now" Willis replied with a broad grin. "Yer lecherous bleeder" Selby retorted. Then as an afterthought he added, "I 'ope to Christ that buggers firing blanks, otherwise Hornchurch is gonna be runnin' alive with a lot of snotty nose little bastards!" However, as the all clear started groping its way through the atmosphere, we all stepped back inside. That's when I remembered what I'd been thinking of earlier. "Yeah that's it!" I suddenly exclaimed. "What's it?" Dave chimed in. "Well Dave I've been tryin' to work out exactly what our bearded friend will do next," I said with a wide grin covering my face. "Christ mate, I thought that bloody obvious, he'll keep movin' about and go on makin' us bleedin' lot look even more stupid than some of us really are". While saying these encouraging words, Dave gave a casual glance in Plumpkin's direction. "No, you misunderstand, see, I'm thinkin' what would I do in his place? I reckon for a start I'd get rid of that bloody fungus round me face, then unless that walkin' cane is a weapon of sorts, I'd lose that too. Anyway whatever, I reckon the bugger will definitely change his lodgings" I made this statement while giving it a considerable amount of thought. Needless to say it was Plumpkin who stepped in next with "Yeah right, I can understand choppin' off that useless growth of 'air under 'is nose, but why get rid of 'is third leg? After all, almost everyone carries a bleedin' stick these days. As for changin' 'is bleedin' lodgings, don't make sense to me" and so ended Plumpkin's observation on the matter.

I first glanced at Plumpkin, then to DI Selby with raised eyebrows. "You're bloody right mate, he's nuts" I whispered, thereby agreeing with Dave's earlier statement. I then turned back to address Plumpkin. "Look mate, 'e 'as to lose that particular stick because it's recognisable and associated with 'im. For instance 'ow many times 'ave we been told our man carries a heavy walkin' stick?" I then waited, no response came back from Plumpkin, so I continued "yer see instead 'e could maybe carry a straight polished cane" I told him, hoping I'd settled that part of any argument at least. Nevertheless, in return I received a somewhat begrudging "Yeah, suppose yer could be right". To which I replied "Oh thanks" I then continued to explain why our bearded man should change his lodgings.

*

It was whilst Reg. Martin carefully removed his beard, then expertly trimmed his moustache, that his landlady explained how she had acquired so much military ordnance, which he, Martin, had discovered earlier. "Well you see, a lot of those bits and pieces were already up there when I moved in early last year, and once or twice a month ever since, this rugged-looking lorry driver pops in with an odd box or two" She thoughtfully informed him. "I see, so that means you've been running a lodging house full of high explosives and with one or two other deadly weapons lying about" Martin summed up. "Have I?" Sally answered in mock 'little girl innocence'. "Yes, I'm afraid you have my darling, and of course, you know what that means don't you?" Martin asked in a knowing way. "No, what does it mean?" Sally naively asked. "Well, with the one or two incidents I've been involved in recently, I've suddenly become a liability to you" Martin stated, hoping Sally would see the logic in what was obvious. "Yes but how can that make any difference? After all, that stuff has been up there a long time, and besides, we're the only ones who know about it" she argued. "Well that means so far you've been lucky, but now if one of those special branch men cotton onto me and chance to follow me back here, sooner or later they will eventually search this house, and that my love will be the end of you," Martin patiently went on to explain. After which he allowed a minute or two of silence to elapse before asking Sally if she could remember who delivered the case that lay on top of the large wardrobe.

"Oh yes, I certainly do, that same rugged bugger who brought the rest of the stuff, he spoke like a real cockney, but I'm sure he originates from Minden, Germany" Sally happily revealed. Martin gave this a moments' thought "The reason I ask is because I've got it in mind that somewhere up there" he gestured upstairs "You must have a bundle of small arms stashed away somewhere, and that case is the only place I didn't look, and from now on I think I'd be well advised to carry a revolver with me, anyway I'll take a further look up there later" Martin concluded.

*

"Don't yer see?" I once again began to repeat myself, having already gone through my well thought out scenario and been argued down by my dear old pal Plumpkin. "'E must know we 'ave a bloody good description of 'im now, so if we get onto where 'e's lodging, 'e must realise the game would be up, for 'im and all 'is playmates, yer know, the buggers' supplying 'im with them bloody grenades and whatnots" I once again explained solely for Plumpkin's benefit. "Wouldn't 'e 'ave brought a few of them bloody grenades with im?" Plumpkin put forward in some doubt. Then by way of a change, DI Selby took over "Don't be a bloody dim wit all yer bleedin' life Jeff" he first raved, then carrying his reasoning forward, lowering the tone of his voice and saying "look me ol; mate, this bugger may well 'ave brought a few bits with 'im, but chances are, place where 'e's lodgin', probably overloaded with all sorts of military paraphernalia, and that's where this buggers supplies are constantly coming from. Now 'ave yer got all that?" Selby forcefully stressed the point. Plumpkin was about to say something, but again was forced to remain silent as DC Willis took a turn at waggling his tongue. "Yeah, I can see what yer getting' at, once we've nabbed 'im, a quick search round 'is lodgings and Bobs yer bleedin' uncle, the whole bleedin' lot would be exposed!" Willis knowingly yet needlessly informed us. "Must say that didn't take us too bloody long to work that out" Selby added for good measure, and also puttin' an end to some brilliantly thought out deductive work.

The Luftwaffe showed up again late that evening, it must have been about 10pm before they put in another appearance. Nevertheless several minutes in advance of any air raid warning, anti-aircraft guns became audible in the far off distance, and as we waited in anticipation for the Hornchurch siren to start wailing, a bomb exploded some distance away blowing open our front door, so naturally we all made a rush in that direction, switching all lights off as we went. After cautiously scouring the area, making sure of no lingering danger, we stood smoking and studying the night sky that was, incidentally, full of searchlights adding a touch more brightness to this already moonlit sky. Although to be fair one searchlight had already netted an enemy bomber, and was tracking him across this bright night sky. There was also dozens of shell bursts leaving black smoke dancing about in the searchlight beam, and of course, we could quite clearly see flashes from distant anti-aircraft guns; that's when the people of Hornchurch became aware of an air raid in progress.

However it was when two heavy explosions occurred around back that I began fearing we might be in trouble. I therefore gave Selby an urgent dig on his arm and said, "I think somethin's wrong round back Dave". He quickly responded "Right, you Willis, 'ave a look-see round back, see everythin's ok," he ordered. Two minutes later Willis was once again beside us. "I think the back rooms gone sir" he nervously reported. "Gone!, what d'yer bloody mean gone?" Dave replied disbelievingly. "Look you wait 'ere, I'll 'ave a butchers me bleedin' self" Dave groaned, and was gone. It took Dave slightly longer before he returned, though in the event, his observations concurred with DC Willis. "He's bloody right, we've lost that bloody back room" he almost repeated Willis's words. Both Plumpkin and I stood in silence for a moment, then I groaned "For Christ sake" and I slipped along the passage to see for myself, and would you believe on entering the room, found myself again studying the night sky, with searchlights and shell bursts dancing about everywhere. "It can't be" I told myself. But there it was, I could see no blackout blinds, just a night sky as mentioned, then a brainwave caressed me, I reached over, found a light switch, I quite deliberately pressed down, with negative results, so like any good soldier caught in this situation I simply said "Fuck it" and rejoined my team mates. "Can't understand that Dave I didn't 'ear anythin' explode that near, did you?" I mumbled. "Oh don't worry it's bloody gone now," Dave replied.

It was whilst Dave Selby and I, along with Willis had been venting our anger at Jerry for trying to re-arrange our living quarters, that Plumpkin meanwhile had, so he'd explained later, out of curiosity wondered along the moonlit passage, ascended a few stairs that lead to an upstairs flat, however when halfway up, for some unknown reason paused a moment to survey the semi-dark passage below him. He was somewhat surprised to find himself looking at two room doors downstairs still intact. He therefore quickly retraced his steps and with help from a near full moon which shone happily through a wide-open front door, where three brilliant detectives still stood cursing Jerry, Plumpkin had opened the first door which he said had been shut tight, after stepping into the room, turned immediately right while bearing in mind what the rest of us had told him about the missing back room, he therefore expected to find himself walking through into the back garden. Instead he'd walked straight into a brick wall, which he severely cursed. Here, DI Selby intervened "Oh, so that was you we 'eard rantin' and ravin' back there," he said giving me a wink. Plumpkin again took over "Course it bloody was, who else? Anyway when I opened the next bloody door, I found myself standin' in a different room altogether. Blackout blinds blowin', French doors wide open." Here Plumpkin's chronicle ended, leaving our imagination to take over. First we stood in complete silence, then in spite of two more bombs exploding nearby, we all burst into a fit of laughter. "What a dozy lot of bleeders we all are, would yer believe, bloody three of us went along that passage, and made the same bloody mistake by going through the wrong door. Missing the first room entirely. What a right balls up," Selby concluded. "Yeah, and ain't yer bloody lucky to 'ave a brilliant MI5 agent on 'and to solve yer bleedin' problem" Plumpkin informed us.

27:

A GUN AND A KISS GOODBYE

Martin replaced the suitcase he'd been sorting through that day, having first removed a 1916 standard service Webley 11 revolver, which he considered to be the ideal weapon for his needs. He also selected an old Webley & Scott 32inch (8mm) automatic pistol that was at times favoured by the Metropolitan police. Martin also reasoned that his landlady Sally, should be in a position to defend herself at all times. He therefore sorted through this array of weaponry, and finally selected a further pistol, a Browning baby standard (6.35-mm) automatic, for her personal protection. Sally at first emphatically refused to have anything to do with firearms of any kind whatsoever, so Martin decided not to argue the point, however he insisted on demonstrating to her how to operate the weapon. He then went on to show her exactly where he had concealed this weapon, at the same time impressing on her that it was simply in case of an emergency. This she agreed to.

That night continuous air raids invoked a restless night for both Reg. Martin and his landlady, in consequence Martin spent best part of that night searching through several street maps, hoping to discover a fresh location for new lodgings. However in the event, it was Sally who solved his problem by mentioning a friend she knew, who would no doubt welcome another lodger. "Oh yes, Dorothy has rather a large house you see, something like six or seven bedrooms and she lets each gentleman rent one room. She does all of their cooking and cleans their rooms, so when they arrive from work they can just relax". "Sounds like just the place I'm looking for" Martin replied, then slowly and thoughtfully added, "No questions asked, I hope?" "Most definitely not" he was told.

It was in the early hours of the morning when they'd got to bed, Sally told him she would nip along and see her friend Dorothy that day, "she's only a bus ride away, and if possible I'll book a room on your behalf". "Good idea, say for about a week" was his response. "Right," Sally said nodding in agreement. "Good mein klein kartoffel," he replied.

*

Early next morning Plumpkin left us saying 'he would be back in a day or two'. DC Willis had of course already returned to his own digs, and no doubt spent what was left of that night cuddled close to his very attractive landlady, while Selby and I lay in bed racked with jealousy. "Lucky bugger" Plumpkin had remarked before he had left.

Anyway DI Selby stepped in as Mother later that morning and quickly cremated four slices of toast, then to cover his misdemeanour smothered the whole bloody lot with lashings of that American concoction 'powdered egg', which they insist is doing us the world of good. "There yer are Bill, get that bleedin' lot down yer" Dave invited. "Oh bloody lovely, where's the bacon?" I asked. "Well I'm glad yer asked that mate, coz it's still rollin' around in the bleedin' mud somewhere," he told me with a toothy grin. After demolishing that ungodly offering, we spent an hour or so sitting about smoking.

While Dave was elaborating on the episode concerning the young office girl who'd been murdered at

Dagenham Cables, our phone suddenly came alive. I cut Dave short in mid-sentence "'Ang on" I said, rushed into the hall and hastily snatched an angry phone off its hook, then someone told me, it wasn't me they wanted. "Put DI Selby on the line" someone growled. However, after five minutes discussion with whoever it was, Dave told me to nip along and pull DC Willis away from his early morning lovemaking session. "Tell 'im we need the bloody car" Dave rattled off. "Why, what's up Dave?" I asked. "You'll see mate, it's back to Dagenham and up to the bloody smoke again" he enlightened me. "Yer mean we're gonna go to London by car?" I hopefully replied. "Maybe" he answered, hustling me out the front door.

As it happened I bumped into Willis halfway along the street. I explained we needed the car. "Why for Christ sake?" he asked in slight irritation. "Coz we're goin' back to where them bleedin' cockneys sound funny, after you've been livin' down 'ere too long" I offered in return. He then informed me he'd taken the bloody car back to Hornchurch police station. "Well now you'll 'ave a nice long walk, won't yer, do yer bleedin' good" I let him know. I then returned to tell DI Selby what had transpired. "Ah bugger it, never mind we'll 'ave a cuppa while waitin'" he patiently rumbled, at the same time indicating that I should be tea boy.

By the time DC Willis arrived back with our chariot, Dave had explained to me how he'd been instructed to first drop in at 22a, Stanley Road, where a Special Branch man should be waiting our arrival. This would be followed by another visit to Dagenham Cables, where we'd be further informed in what direction this investigation would be going from now on. We'll also be involved in another trip to Kent, this time a place called Warlingham, this on account of some well-informed citizen who'd apparently walked into a Kent police station and calmly given them a description of our bearded warrior, who he'd seen, and had somehow known that we were in fact looking for such a man. At this point Dave's narrative was cut short by DC Willis giving a long heavy blast on the motor horn.

Minutes later we pushed through the front gate in Stanley Road. On this occasion I made sure to be last in entering, just in case that new bloody spring was still playing tricks. It was, but this time I was ready for the bloody thing, and far too dexterous for it. My old mate Selby patted my back. "Well done Bill" he praised, then turned, took one step forward, caught the heel of his shoe on a miscellaneous brick, which no doubt had been lobbed over by some local 'hard nut'. In performing this action Dave could not help but give DC Willis, who had preceded him, an almighty shove in the back, thereby sending him headfirst through a then wide-open front door, while DI Selby himself gave a grand display on how to flatten one's nose on someone's front doorstep. And of course, after this event, they both sat together on the doorstep offering their appreciation to the Gods for allowing them to enter a house in such a graceful manner, and only receiving a bloody nose each into the bargain. Quite naturally, this incident gave rise to many fits of laughter from several passers-by. I personally removed the offending obstacle by placing it under a row of evergreens. I then entered the house, leaving DI Selby and DC Willis sitting there both feeling sorry for themselves.

*

Reg. Martin made a point of concealing the Webley Revolver in his waistband under his jacket. Satisfied himself it couldn't be seen, he then gave Sally a kiss, at the same time accepting an envelope which bore the name and address of Sally's friend Dorothy. Sally had previously explained to Martin that Dorothy allowed each of her tenants a front door key and had no qualms about the comings and goings. "Oh yes, just one more thing, she also has a rule of never getting involved with any of her male residents" Sally further informed him with a knowing grin. For an answer she received a wide smile and another kiss before the door closed behind him.

Martin was led into Dorothy's parlour, supplied with a cigarette, asked to sit and relax while she made a fresh pot of tea. It was here Martin began to wonder if he'd been perhaps a little hasty in his decision to leave Sally. In any case one thing he was certain of, Dorothy was a very attractive voluptuous woman, who could excite any man. She was in fact a very desirable lady who possessed a great deal of sexual charm, with what appeared to be a permanent sun tanned skin, long black hair, with soft brown eyes that from the moment they looked at you, seemed to be begging you to join her in bed. This he realised was why Sally had made a point of telling him Dorothy would have no truck involving herself with her tenants. 'My God' Martin thought, 'if she did, every red-blooded male would be craving her favours'. Nevertheless Martin sat patiently sipping tea while Dorothy, now sitting opposite him, explained how she ran her home. When she finally came to what Martin considered a frustrating narrative of her 'dos and don'ts' their eyes locked, and Martin felt a sudden urge of sexual desire run through him, whereas Dorothy for her part became aware of just how handsome her new lodger was. Dorothy broke the spell by standing, moving to the far end of this immaculately clean long room. She took a solitary key from a mahogany sideboard draw, she then handed Martin said key, which he gratefully accepted with a certain amount of relief. It was however as he took the key their hands touched and Martin became aware of a slight change in Dorothy's attitude. It was as though a barrier between them had been lifted. He then realised this beautiful liquid brown-eyed creature was about to break her own golden rule, and when she also invited him to have tea with her that evening, Martin knew he had succeeded in winning this sexy young lady over.

28:

NEW LODGINGS

22a, Stanley Road was the last place I expected to find our old mate from the 1916 battlefield, but to my surprise there he stood again, ready and waiting to shake hands with me, our old pal John Wakeman. "Well I'll be buggered, where on earth did you come from?" I asked in amazement while accepting his outstretched hand. "I'd have thought you would have guessed that by now Bill, us Special Branch boys are taking over from your lot now" He informed me, he then went on to ask where Sgt: Selby was "he's still with you, I take it Bill?" I grinned back at him "Yes he is, and don't let 'im 'ear yer say 'Sgt:' Selby, those days 'ave long gone mate and 'e's now known as DI Selby from Scotland Yard, and I'm 'is bleedin' Sergeant to boot, understand Johnny me boy?" I corrected him. "Blimey Bill I knew all that" he told me. "Well that's good, just bear that in mind when yer speak to Dave" I reminded him, then went on to say "anyway what d'yer find out about the bloke who got 'imself killed in this place?" whilst pointing over Johnny's shoulder to where Danny Ross's body had been found. "Oh yes, apparently he was an enemy agent and it appears he had a falling out with a fellow conspirator for some reason. Still at any rate we now know our quarry is living somewhere near, or in Warlingham itself" Here I broke in on his speech with "Yeah, we've just found that out ourselves". "Right, in that case you'll be pleased to hear, that's where my lots off to next" he rattled off. "Cor blimey, there's a bloody coincidence, coz Dave said that's exactly where we'll be goin'" I informed him.

Finally Dave Selby and Tony Willis pushed through the door. "Well I'll be buggered, where the bleedin' 'ell did you come from?" Dave exclaimed when he clamped eyes on Johnny Wakeman. They both clasped hands, then Dave introduced Willis, and while they shook hands, Johnny offered Willis some sound advice. "Whatever you do mate keep an eye on those two devious bleeders, otherwise they'll lead you into all sorts of trouble, so be warned my old china" Johnny's offering was sincerely laid out, as though it was Dave and I and not Tony who was having it off with our landlady. Nevertheless he did manage a cunning wink for us while saying it. "Right, that's it then, now I'm off" Johnny announced. "Christ, yer ain't been 'ere 'alf a minute" Selby protested. "Sorry mate but I really must go, Billy here will bring you up to date on things" he informed Selby, as more hand shaking followed. Then he was gone. Next Selby came at me with "Ok Bill what's goin' on then. I bet that sods up to somethin' we should know about" Selby guessed. "Well all I can say is, 'e told me 'is lot 'Special Branch' are off to Warlingham, where they've been informed our bearded warrior is now livin'". "So ol' Johnny Wakeman is 'Special Branch' is he? He always was a clever bleeder that one" Selby retorted, then added "Still never mind, I've been told we're now just investigatin' the murders, so from 'ere Dagenham Cables is our next port of call" Dave relayed this piece of news with a forlorn sound ringing in his voice.

Willis and I both gave a grunt, Dave then added "and no matter what, I've been instructed, after Dagenham, it's back to London and then onto Warlingham, so 'ave no illusions Bill, this bloke we're lookin' for now in regards to these three murders, I 'ave no doubt will turn out to be our friendly saboteur, that RAF corporal from Old Ford Road, remember? The same bugger who's 'ad us runnin' around like blue arse flies for bleedin' days now" Dave Selby summarised. "Well at least we know what we're doin' for once" I passed onto DC Willis who just nodded.

*

When Reg. Martin arrived back at Dorothy's house with two suitcases, he'd already made sure they contained no offensive weapons, in fact the only weapon he possessed at that moment was the Webley revolver, which he kept snugly tucked away in his waistband. Dorothy greeted him with a welcoming smile. On closing the front door behind him, she also relieved him of the smaller of his suitcases. "This way," she said heading for a flight of stairs "you have a room opposite the bathroom, my room's next door" she purposely pointed out with a faint smile. "Oh I see," Martin managed while struggling with the larger suitcase. "Right here we are, in here" she softly murmured on opening a room door. "Looks fine to me," Martin remarked agreeably. "Good I'll give you a list of times for meals and so on later" she then promised. He just answered with a smile. As she was about to leave the room, she suddenly pulled up sharp, "Oh yes, by the way, don't forget you're joining me for tea, say around eight this evening, I should be through by then" she reminded him. "Great I'll be there" was all he could think to say.

For an hour or so Martin lay on his bed, contemplating what he should do next. He realised of course that just knowing Dorothy sympathised with him, was not enough in itself. No, he must be absolutely sure she was one hundred per cent in favour of what he stood for. She must in fact be like Sally, whom he could rely on at all times in any situation. Martin also knew the best way to insure this was to win her affections, and as everyman knows there's only one sure way to achieve this, and that is to get her into bed quickly and make your lovemaking last as long as possible, then impress upon her it was not just sex alone, there is a real genuine affection you feel for her. Of course she'll not believe a word you're saying, but hopefully your tender lovemaking will have won the day and of course she will like to hear you say, 'how much you enjoyed having sex with such a beautiful woman'.

All these thoughts going through Martins mind caused him to suddenly burst into an uncontrollable fit of laughter, as he realised that's probably exactly what she was expecting him to do that night. After a while however the humour deserted him, when he also realised his new landlady possessed all the attributes that could in fact make many a man really seek her favours.

*

As I closed the front door in Stanley Road and headed towards a fast closing front gate, which DI Selby had left wide open leaving said gate to swing shut under its own steam, Selby and Willis having both preceded me, I was once again accosted by my scruffy snotty nose little urchin from across the road. This time however, I needed no decoding machine, he spoke in perfect English. "Oi mister, where yer been? 'ere, last time I saw yer, you and that other bloke both wore bleedin' turbins round yer bonses, wot were yer, in bleedin' disguise or sumick?" he rattled off for half the street to hear. I immediately gave him a threatening look. "No son we wasn't in disguise, some bugger had given us a nasty bang on our 'eads, and some 'elpfull Doctor said we must wear a bandage for a while" I explained to the little feller light-heartedly. "Blimey wasn't that bloke who done that bleedin' murder, was it?" He eloquently expressed himself. "Could 'ave been 'im" I answered. "Course it was, bet it bleedin' 'urt, taught yer a sodden lesson though, anyway I'm orf, see yer" he informed me before skipping happily down the road to greet his mates.

I caught up with Selby and Willis at Hornchurch police station. "We still got a bleedin' car ain't we?" I straight away asked Selby. He answered in the affirmative, then "Where you been all this time?" He enquired. I thereupon reiterated what my snotty-nosed well informed little friend had recited for me. "Knowin' little bugger, I reckon if we 'ung around 'ere long enough he'd solve the bloody case for us" Selby said jokingly.

About ten minutes later we received tea and biscuits from a disgruntled desk sergeant. He apologised for only being able to offer us such a meagre offering "It's the bleedin' rationing" he complained, then went on to explain just how low the station was on supplies, and would not receive further supplies until the Romford Super sent in a request". "And when will that be?" Selby enquired. "Well it's like this sir, doesn't really matter to him, because he gets a separate allowance" the sergeant told us in confidence. "Oh I see, well never mind sergeant," Selby exonerated him. "That's very nice of you sir" the sergeant offered by way of a thank you. "That's alright sergeant, anyway we'll be leaving any minute now" Selby informed him. I guessed in the hope of stopping the poor sod from any more worrying.

Tea time over, Selby then took it upon himself to give Willis and me a run down on what we would be doing next. So now as all three of us sat smoking, our DI began to give his two junior partners the low down.

*

That evening Dorothy surprised Reg. Martin by placing in front of him a powdered egg and mushroom omelette on a plate with an assortment of lettuce, spring onions, tomatoes and cucumber as a side salad. "How on earth did you manage this?" he openly enquired with obvious praise in his voice. "Well my dear man it's mostly from my garden, don't you know" she answered proudly.

However, it was later while they sat on a plush sofa enjoying a cigarette that Dorothy broached the subject of his employment. "Now come on, you really must tell me all about yourself and there's no need to fabricate, Sally has already very discreetly given me some idea of what you do, so there, you can be quite frank with me" she advised. It took a moment or two while Martin sat in stunned silence and completely lost for words. Nevertheless after a while he glanced at her with devilment written across his face. "So tell me, what exactly did Sally say about me?" he enquired mischievously.

29:

RETURN TO SCOTLAND YARD

As it turned out going to Dagenham had been a waste of time, and of course, the moment we arrived back in London a bloody air-raid siren started wailing again, so instead of sitting in a comfortable armchair inside Scotland Yard discussing our next move, we were instead all three of us seated, cuddling a mug of hot tea, around an old dilapidated table, on some 'Utility' chairs in one of those new community bloody damp flimsy brick-built street air raid shelters, that seemed to be springing up everywhere since the blitz started. And of course by taking refuge in this particular shelter, we were still some distance away from Scotland Yard itself, and by the way Dave and I were dithering about, all three of us must have been giving a bloody good impersonation of 'The Three Stooges'. Anyway after so much buggering about, our leader DI Selby took the floor. "Right lads" he began as though addressing a whole bloody battalion of men "this is 'ow it goes so far and 'ere we take a step back in time, yer see, it all started with that clever bastard Danny Ross, who as we all now know started the ball rollin' by takin' us for a stroll up the bloody garden path" Dave broke off, gave Willis and yours truly a knowing smile, plus a cigarette each. He then released two smoke rings around our brick-built shack, and I sensed this monologue of his was gonna be one of them late-night sessions. I therefore accordingly leant my chair back against the wall, on its two back legs of course, I carefully put my feet upon the table, gently closed my eyes, waiting patiently for Dave to begin his sermon. Instead I went arse over tip when my bloody war time 'Utility' chair collapsed beneath me, I then sat on the floor listening to Selby and Willis laughing their bollocks off. Nevertheless like most Londoners at that time, according to Winston Churchill, I knew I could take it, so I thereupon offered one or two sincere chosen words to my partners, pulled myself to my feet and amongst several more fits of laughter grabbed another one of them bloody 'Utility' chairs, then puffing hard on a fresh cigarette, re-seated myself, only this time showing more respect to the bloody half-baked war time contraption I was sitting on.

Dave wiping tears from his eyes started again. "Right, after that very entertaining interlude, I will resume. Now it would seem once Danny Ross had served his purpose, which was to make us think Hornchurch aerodrome was going to be the Luftwaffe's main target, they quickly decided to rid themselves of 'im, get rid of 'im completely. So that's murder number one we can put down to our RAF corporal, on account 'e was seen in the area. Next we discover an RAF sergeant who, by the way, appeared to have been seen givin' an RAF corporal a lift, then sometime later the sergeants body is found and we're told he too 'ad been murdered. So once again we can place our corporal in the frame for murder number two. Now we come to Dagenham Cables and that poor young lady who copped it there". At this point Dave sighed, gave Willis and myself a critical glance, dowsed his half-smoked cigarette under his foot, then started in again. "Ok, we now know that some gent with a bearded face carrying a heavy walkin' stick was observed in that vicinity, and of course sometime later our brilliant MI5 agent, dear ol' Plumpkin, does the light fantastic with some codger in that Heathway tobacconist. The feller he's waltzing with incidentally is wearing a neatly trimmed beard and also as we all saw, was clutching a heavy walking stick and I'm betting this bugger is in fact that same bloody RAF corporal, only 'avin' deserted the RAF, is now posing as an old gentleman about town. Nevertheless I'm convinced that young lady's death can also be put down to 'im as murder number three"

Here Dave was suddenly cut short, as we all three claimed a space under the table, as a string of bombs whistled down and exploded too near for comfort. At the same time, we heard lots of light 'pings' hitting the ground, followed by what seemed to sound like several humming tops spinning merrily away, while also making a hissing sound. Of course we knew this could only be attributed to dozens of incendiary bombs designed to create fires, and very successful they had been so far. And of course when you have a couple of dozen fire bombs to deal with, believe me, the last thing you need is a string of high explosive bombs exploding all over the place.

*

Reg. Martin now clean-shaven, just a neatly trimmed moustache left in place, his heavy walking stick also discarded, had decided to first take a long walk around his new surroundings. This in order to familiarise himself with the area in which he now lodged. The night before he had delayed giving Dorothy a straight answer regarding his profession, until they'd been in bed for an hour or so. After which he confessed everything. As it turned out, she'd promised her full support, and help in any way possible. So after making love to her again that night, he knew she would stand by him no matter what.

Martin returned to his lodgings after a long enjoyable walk. He now dwelt in one of several rather old, yet larger properties that dotted the landscape here about. Probably 'Edwardian' he thought, and funny enough these properties all faced towards a small village which consisted of, the usual post office, pub, butchers, and of course the local grocery shop, but to Martins delight was completely void of a police station. On his way back, he had also observed these dwellings were completely surrounded by open fields. On opening the front door with his new key, he found Dorothy had prepared a meal in his absence, which consisted of one kipper and two slices of buttered brown bread. Martin also noticed that the two or three other lodgers that were staying with Dorothy, were at this time of day at their place of work. While devouring his meal, she sat talking to him. She began by explaining how her husband had in fact been born in Dusseldorf, Germany. Having been brought to England as a child, always considered himself to be British and therefore, when war broke out, he immediately enlisted in the British army, and she was very proud of him, and everything Britain stood for. That's until Winston Churchill sent him along with three or four thousand other riflemen to Calais, France, in order to prevent German armour flooding into Dunkirk, where the remanet of the British army were then trapped. Of course, as expected Dorothy was by now in tears. Martin knowing all the facts, finished the story for her. "Yes I know my dear, about three thousand English soldiers were sacrificed in that fiasco," he said sympathetically. She wiped her eyes, blew her nose then added "Yes, that great Englishman sacrificed all those men and for what" she groaned, giving Martin a pleading glance, then added "my poor Eric was so proud and eager to go" she finally murmured as he placed a comforting arm around her shoulders. "Come my dear, don't upset yourself" he pacified.

*

Whilst seated in the canteen of this edifice building called Scotland Yard, where coincidentally DI Selby and I his sergeant, shared a small office from time to time. However, at this particular moment, we were being waited on by a PC Holden who had been given the task of seeing we received an adequate meal, as we all sat expressing our relief on having vacated that bloody council brick-built street air-raid shelter. Nonetheless as we sat stuffing ourselves with beans on toast, that poxy air raid warning started wailing yet again. This time our anti-aircraft guns were quick off the mark, so like half the residents of Scotland Yard, we rushed outside for a look-see, and because it was a sunny afternoon, we could see quite clearly why our guns were so quick. A group of about fifty jerry bombers blackened the London sky. It was quite obvious our guns were trying to keep jerry busy until our fighter aircraft could take over, which wasn't too long.

As it turned out, our ground guns suddenly quit and just as suddenly machine gun fire could be heard overhead. Several Hurricanes were seen darting through an enemy formation, then Selby and I heard Willis yell in despair "Oh for Christ sake, look at that bleedin' lot" he pointed to a group of Messerschmitt 109's flying slightly above our Hurricanes, and as we watched they began peeling off to attack our fighters who were truly outnumbered. "Blimey, that's their bleedin' fighter escort" Selby announced. Meanwhile I'd spotted a squadron of Spitfires about to enter the fray. I pointed in front of the Luftwaffe bombers and quickly drew Selby and Willis's attention to them by calmly saying "Wait till Jerry meets them bleedin' bunch of boys". I was immediately answered by DC Willis "Christ, where'd that lot come from?" he yelled in amazement. "Ain't got a bloody clue mate, but it evens things up, don't it!" I replied delightedly, as we stood watching several individual dog fights break out across a fairly bright late afternoon sky. At this point many of Scotland Yards' personnel were standing outside cheering our boys on, that's until the bombs started raining down. Then surprisingly enough they all performed a quick disappearing act, leaving just three silly buggers outside still cheering.

30:

A FAST TRIP TO WARLINGHAM

When DI Selby instructed DC Willis to drive us to Warlingham fast, I was amazed at the urgency and his exuberance, and what's more I don't recall ever witnessing this attitude in Dave's demeanour before, but in any case when I asked why the rush, he simply smiled at me, then in a voice that confirmed his seniority said, "That Billy me boy is on a need to know basis, and you don't need to know right now". So I thanked him for showing so much confidence in his old pal, and showed him two fingers.

It was our driver DC Willis who broke up this spell of banter between Dave and me by slamming down hard on the brakes and skidding to a halt. He immediately apologised with "Oops, sorry sir, bloody squirrel," while us two silly sods sitting in back hung on for dear life. "What the bleedin' 'ell yer tryin' to do, kill us or what?" Selby stormed. "Not really sir, but a squirrel ran across the road in front us sir" Willis offered in defence. Seeing Dave was about to have another go at him, I quickly stepped in on Willis's behalf "Bloody excitin' though Dave, wasn't it?" I merrily sung out, not being able to think of anything better to say, and still suffering the trauma of nigh on being thrown through the windscreen, I guess made my thinking a bit slow. Anyway Dave Selby just gave me a blank stare, then leaning calmly forward advised Willis to drive a touch more careful in future, and if necessary in future kill the bloody squirrel, "the government want to get rid of them anyway" Dave informed him. So once again we were off on our way to Warlingham.

*

That same morning Reg. Martin stepped outside the front door of his new lodgings. He took a deep breath and happily studied a clear blue sky. At this point he felt quite confident within himself. For a start his new landlady Dorothy had accepted him as her lover, and also committed herself to his cause. Having already retrieved the Webley & Scott automatic pistol he'd previously left at Sally's house, while leaving behind several other deadly devices.

Reg. Martin began a brisk walk heading towards the small village. As he did so he was focusing on his next mission, he at first considered a trip back to Dagenham to deal with that chemical factory 'May & Baker' along with 'Ever Ready' battery firm. However, after giving this action some serious consideration, he realised he had in fact neglected to give any more thought as to what he should do concerning the Hornchurch aerodrome. After all this was to be his first priority until that idiot Danny Ross, his fellow conspirator, had taken it upon himself to interfere by telling the police he'd seen someone taking photographs of Hornchurch airfield. Thereby trying to delude the police into thinking that Hornchurch was under threat from saboteurs and by doing this had disrupted all of Martins plans. Nevertheless that problem having now been dealt with, Martin could see no reason for neglecting that airfield any longer, who knows, he might even be able to make one or two slight alterations concerning their airfield layout. Here, Martins train of thought was interrupted when a soft voice behind him suggested he should slow down a trifle. Martin stopped abruptly, turned and was amazed to see Sally, his ex-landlady staring up at him. "Oh my dear lady, how are you?" he enquired in a sensitive manner. "Well my love, I'm alright, I just slipped over to warn you, there are several policemen roaming this area now, knocking on doors and asking us landladies if we'd taken in any new lodgers recently. Just thought you should know my dear" she explained. "Ah right, thank you for telling me, but don't worry, I'll be away from here by morning, and when I get back, I'll pop round and see you. Will that be alright?" he said hoping to put Sally's mind at ease. "Oh yes, that would be alright, but nonetheless it occurred to me, you might need these" Sally told him, at the same time handing him a medium-size canvas shopping bag "There's about twenty of those time delayed things in there" she whispered confidentially.

*

Once again we found ourselves in an old shack that the locals in Warlingham considered to be a first-class police station. Anyway be that as it may, after a rather long laborious drive down from London DI Selby, me and DC Willis, had settled ourselves in a quiet little room in this happy little shack, where they had by the way, rolled out the welcoming mat for us in as much as offering us tea and biscuits, and a friendly sergeant even supplied us with cigarettes. It was a bit later after we'd sampled all these goodies, that a sergeant took us along and introduced us to the areas Assistant Chief Constable Roberts, who had the dubious task of bringing us up to date on where his team were quite sure they had located the area in which one or two enemy agents were now operating from. He'd handed

Dave a sheet of paper which contained a small map with street names to one side of it. "There you are Inspector" the ACC said whilst pointing to a turning named Nelson Road "about halfway down that road you'll find a detached house, you can't miss it, painted dark green, and it's the only detached property in that turning. Anyway we've had it under surveillance for about a week now, and we're convinced there's some sort of unlawful activity going on inside" he knowingly informed DI Selby, who nodded his head, gave a little cough, offered me a shrug before turning back to ACC Roberts, and clearly stated "Yes, well I understand all that Sir, but with respect Sir the thing is, you see Sir, we've been sent here as part of our investigation, which involves three murders only, and as you know Sir, one of the victims was an RAF Sergeant, who happened to be stationed down here at Biggin Hill. So you see, unless we can be assured that there is a connection between the person we're looking for in respect of the three murders and those people you refer to in Nelson Road, I'm afraid my team and I must first pay the Biggin Hill Aerodrome a visit Sir" Selby made this statement in a truly professional manner while standing to attention the whole time. Did a smart about turn and indicated we should now leave.

However, ACC Roberts was not quite through "Right in that case Inspector Selby I'll give you my personal assurance, that all here are convinced that at least one amongst them living there is in fact your man, now I will say no more. I'll leave it entirely up to you, as to what you do next" and with that ACC Roberts made a dismissive gesture, an obvious invitation for us to leave.

*

Reg. Martin instinctively knew he was now being watched, although realising he had no real evidence to support this, he nevertheless decided to take no unnecessary chances. He therefore selected six time-delayed grenades from those Sally had given him earlier. The rest he reasoned would be safe enough tucked away somewhere in Dorothy's garden air-raid shelter. Having explained all this to Dorothy, Martin then coaxed her into his bedroom by way of a change, where they stayed until nightfall. He then told Dorothy to open the front door. "And do what?" she asked. "It doesn't really matter my love" he began, then as an afterthought added "light a cigarette maybe, just draw attention to yourself in case anyone's watching the house, and I'll be able to slip out of the back door unnoticed," he told her with a pat on her backside to help her along, and as he'd surmised some ten seconds after Dorothy opened the front door, a gruff voice shouted "Put that bloody light out!"

By this time however, Martin had closed the back door, leapt over the fence at the bottom of Dorothy's garden and was standing in a side alley which led into a field. Cutting across said field he knew would take him into Sally's street and in fact right passed her house. Strange as it may seem, when he finally arrived back in that street which was in fact Nelson Road, where he'd previously lodged with Sally, he felt completely safe, free from any anxiety he'd had about being watched whilst at Dorothy's. This fear became a thing of the past. Walking passed Sally's front door, in spite of the darkness, Martin clearly saw several ARP wardens roaming about. However, what really amazed him was when a fuel tanker drew alongside him, and a voice from within called "I say old chap, you wouldn't be going my way by any chance". Automatically, Martins guard was up. He cautiously peered into a completely dark cab, with suspicion, but suddenly, a small cab light flickered on for a second, just long enough to reveal a face Martin clearly recognised as that of the tanker driver, who not long ago had driven him to Warlingham and had also given him Sally's address. In any case Martin having changed his mind again, climbed into the cab telling the driver he was on his way to Dagenham. "Ah, that's alright then, coz I'm carrying a load for Hornchurch aerodrome". Martin nodded his appreciation, sat back in the passenger seat and relaxed. He then slowly took and lit a cigarette from his pocket, offered one to this friendly driver, and while holding a light for him, Martin casually asked, "How did you know where to find me this time my friend?" The driver gave him a side on glance and a small belly laugh before answering "Oh, so you realise it was me gave you a lift from Folkestone some time ago". "That's right, you also gave me Sally's address and I seem to remember the name 'Red' cropping up, is that right?" Martin queried. "You are quite right my friend, I am 'Red' and by the way it was Sally herself told me to now look out for you, and to inform you that her house is now under surveillance, so you are safer at Dorothy's for the moment. Although we're guessing you were under the impression it was Dorothy's house being watched". Martin was amazed at this revelation and replied by stating "But I had no idea, I'm sure it was Dorothy's house being watched". "Yes, we thought you might think that" at this point Martin cut in "but why would you think that?" Red gave a small belly laugh, leant forward and said "You do realise these women do communicate" he reminded him before adding "Oh yes she also ordered me to stay close to you at all times" Red informed him. At this statement Martin looked slightly puzzled and immediately asked "What do you mean, she 'ordered' you! who is she then, to be able to order you to do these things?" Martin then fell silent waiting for Red to respond. However, the answer he finally received, was not at all to his liking, Red simply replied with "My friend, it is more than my, or even your, life is worth for me to tell you that!"

31:

TOO LATE – AGAIN

After a moment or two reflection on what ACC Roberts had said, DI Selby discarded our trip to Biggin Hill aerodrome for the time being, and instead decided he and DC Willis should first take a stroll down Nelson Road, in order to see if we were in fact in any sort of position to apprehend our man, if he was indeed inside this house that ACC Roberts spoke of. Selby's reason for leaving me behind, taking Willis with him instead, was quite reasonable I thought. It was simply on account that if our man was by chance lodging in that house, and happen to see me walk by the front door, having already encountered me at Biggin Hill aerodrome a few days ago, he would know at once we were on to him and that's something Selby wanted to avoid, so we could hopefully catch our man completely off guard when we decided to strike. Now for the time being to minimise showing any suspicion on our part, Dave sent DC Willis off to find a local stall holder who was prepared to let the police borrow (at a price of course) his barrow for a while. Ten minutes later DC Willis returned, mission accomplished. "Right, now you Tony, cop 'old of the bloody barrow, that's it, now you'll be pushin' it along Nelson Road, I'll be walkin' beside yer. Once outside the bloody green 'ouse, I'll stop yer, offer yer a fag. Now while we're lightin' up, you'll say somethin' bloody funny, and we'll both burst out laughin'. Got that?" Selby broke off there, gave Willis a very serious look before continuing "now Tony at that moment we'll both be leanin' on yer ol' barrow laughin' our bollocks off, but our eyes will be takin' in every detail concerning that den of iniquity. Now 'ave yer got all that me ol' son?" Selby asked with a slight chuckle, for DC Willis had already created a round of laughter, simply by tying a red bandana around his neck and placing a peak cap on his head, sideways. "Well at least 'e looks the part Dave," I told Selby "Yeah right" he answered with a small grin. "Come on yer daft bugger, let's get goin'.

*

Sally, Reg. Martins previous landlady, glanced out of the front room window, and happened, to notice two barrow boys walking by. As she did so, one of them said something and they suddenly stop to light a cigarette. Then the other one said something and both burst into a fit of laughter. Sally herself could not help but smile at their antics. Nevertheless at that moment she remembered what Martin had once told her about being wary of strangers, although now as she watched these two men Sally consoled herself with the knowledge that he, Martin her lover, had long fled the area, and should by now be well away from here.

Martin was in fact at that moment walking out of Dagenham Railway Station. He'd left his friendly tanker driver 'Red' at Barking where Martin hopped on a train straight through to Dagenham. Once outside the station, he quickly learnt that May & Baker chemical firm wasn't too far away. In fact as he walked down a slight incline away from said station, he could actually see May & Baker over to his right, it was surrounded by a wire fence.

However, seeing as at that moment an air-raid siren was groaning out the last notes of a warning, Martin therefore considered it to be a good idea to stay far away from any factories for a while. He in fact reasoned this time in the morning wasn't a good time to go anywhere near a chemical plant at all. So for the time being having satisfied himself he was now familiar with the surrounding area, he headed straight on down a long wide road, where some helpful soul had told him to turn right at the far end, and there he would find Ever Ready Battery firm on his immediate left, which he did. By then heavy anti-aircraft gun-fire was ravishing the sky and a squadron or two of German bombers could be seen clawing their way slowly towards London. So once again Martin decided to forego the pleasure of re-arranging another factory, instead he retraced his steps back to Dagenham station. He had it in mind on taking a train to Upminster Bridge. Having been there once before, he knew he could either hop on a bus into Hornchurch village or even walk the couple of miles, would make no difference. He could then no doubt spend an hour or so in a village tea room. After which he might even spend another hour or two in the local 'Odeon' cinema, a somewhat clean looking building which was referred to as the 'Towers'

On reaching Upminster Bridge station, Martin now carrying no walking cane of any kind, decided he would take a brisk walk back to Hornchurch village. Having obtained a row of medal ribbons from Sally's collection of military hardware, which he now had displayed just above his breast pocket of his jacket, indicated he'd served in the British forces at sometime or other. Martin pulled back his shoulders and began a proud walk to Hornchurch. He had convinced himself that a brisk walk would be more beneficial than jumping on a bus. It would also take time, thereby shaving a touch more time off having to spend hanging around in a village tea shop.

*

I think it fair to say that it was the rest of us who was standing either end of Nelson Road, watching DI Selby and DC Willis as they stopped to light a cigarette and suddenly burst into laughter, that could appreciate their performance best. As it was we were all taking this lesson in observation quite seriously, until DC Willis started his laughing routine. He first sat on a handle of the barrow doubled over with laughter, then pulled himself up, then sauntered round and leant on the highest part of the barrow, and while still laughing, actually flung his whole body across it, and of course the bloody barrow went down with a crash, taking him with it, eventually leaving poor old Willis lying sprawled out in the middle of a freshly tarmacked road, with the barrow doing a half leap and rolling completely out of his reach, thus causing DI Selby to first jump to one side, then to make a desperate grab for the bloody barrow. However, what caused us onlookers an even greater laugh was that Selby had no need to grab for the bloody thing at all. It had already stopped, and Selby, silly sod was left sitting on his arse in the middle of the road.

Nevertheless in spite of all this performance they were having with the barrow, I kept a close eye on DI Selby, and could clearly see he was taking in every detail of the green house we had under surveillance, and true to form the moment he'd seen enough he indicated to Willis it was time for them to leave. They both regained their feet,

Willis again taking charge of the barrow and both vacated Nelson Road with smiling faces.

On reaching me and a few other coppers who we'd taken along with us, just in case, Selby glanced at me, gave a slow shake of his head. "The only bloody person I saw in there was a bloody woman, and all she did was laugh at us pair of bleedin' idiots piss balling about with a barrow," Dave said in disappointment. "Well perhaps yer got the wrong 'ouse mate' I replied sympathetically.

*

On relinquishing his seat in the 'Towers' cinema in Hornchurch, Martin checked his watch, calculated he'd been in there for about three hours. Having seen roughly about one and a half films, Martin had fallen into a deep sleep. Next thing he knew, they were playing the National Anthem and everyone was standing. He quickly jumped to his feet, stood to attention in respect, after which he made a point of being last out of said cinema. Once outside, he noticed the sky was now beginning to darken. Martin also noticed something else, a small scruffy boy, and somehow he had a strange feeling he knew this scruffy little kid from somewhere. It then dawned on him where he'd seen this nuisance of a child before. He straight away tried to avoid the kid, but to no avail, for as Martin began to lengthen his stride in order to avoid having any contact whatsoever with this small bundle of joy, Martin suddenly felt himself go cold inside, when a young cockney voice beside him sung out "Oi mister, I know yer, don't I? Yeah, you're that bloke that come ou' that 'ouse, where that bloke was murdered, aintcha?" Martin looked down at his tormentor and remarked, "Shouldn't you be in bloody bed by now?"

Martin then ignored the kid completely and kept on walking as the small voice remarked, "'Ere, yer lucky my dad aint 'ere".

32:

A MERRY DANCE

Our investigation continued, but a week or so later we hadn't got any further. The uniform police carried on with their house to house enquiries, yet so far to date no further progress had been made there. DI Selby and yours truly had a couple more meetings with ACC Roberts, who strongly suggested we now turn our attention back to London, or even Hornchurch might be a better idea. However later that same night whilst crouching in a bloody Anderson garden air-raid shelter back in London's Bow Road, Dave Selby put it to me that although this bugger we're looking for had been taking us for a merry bleedin' dance all over the place, he hadn't yet touched the Hornchurch aerodrome, nor so far had he interfered with May & Baker, that chemical firm in Dagenham. I stood for a moment pondering on what Dave had said. I then chimed in with "What about that battery factory Ever Ready?" "Yeah there, that's another factory" Dave replied as we both automatically ducked when two more bombs exploded close by. Five minutes after which an all clear started whining out its mournful notes.

We'd been cramped up for so long in that bloody air-raid shelter, that it took Dave and I a good fifteen minutes to get our limbs functioning again. Anyway, now back inside the house where my parents still lived, although as it happened they'd gone on holiday to Somerset visiting friends. Selby flicked on the radio and within a couple of minutes we were listening to a repeat broadcast, which was recorded in 1939, of the Lightweight title fight between Eric Boon the British Lightweight champion and his challenger Arthur Danahar. Raymond Glendenning the commenter was screaming his lungs out telling us the Danahar boy had got tagged and gone down. It was at this point while I stirred our tea, Dave supplied us with a cigarette each, that W. Barrington Dalby began his inter-round summary. He started by telling us that our London boy from Bethnal Green had now been down three times. He then reiterated something about the fighting Danahar brothers, those famous boys, and what they were doing for the boxing fraternity. Then quite suddenly a bell rang and they were at it again, with Glendening telling us their every move. "Oh brilliant" he raved "Boon has just made Danahar miss with a vicious right hand". So this is what we sat listening to for fourteen hard-fought rounds before Dave switched this exciting fight off. He then turned to me and said, "That's it Billy me boy, it's back to Dagenham for us". I immediately glanced at him, could see at once he'd had a brainwave. "Come on, we'll hop a train" he rattled off with urgency. "Alright let's get me bleedin' coat on and make sure we turn everything off and make sure the 'ouse is secure" I cautioned him as we hurried from room to room checking everything was in order.

*

As Martin hurried away from the 'Towers' cinema, and the troublesome small boy in particular, he received many suspicious looks from various people, and although it was getting dark, one man amongst them could not help but take a second closer look at this tall figure striding away from this very curious crowd. He nudged his wife walking by his side. "I know that feller, last time I saw him was at

Hornchurch station. He's a corporal, RAF, name of Fletcher I believe" the Hornchurch ticket collector declared to his wife. "Well, so what? He's probably got leave, nothing wrong with him going to the pictures, is there?" she said in this strangers defence. "No no, you don't understand my dear, that young kid just stated, that man was in a house where someone was murdered, and when I took his ticket the other day, he was acting bloody suspicious then" the ticket collector managed to say before his wife impatiently told him "Well in that case, you should ring the police my dear" she offered this statement with some obvious annoyance, then added "now come on, let's get home, in case jerry starts again tonight". "Alright, I'll ring them from home," he told her.

Martin stepped off a number 66 bus at Hornchurch station and immediately started walking towards Hornchurch aerodrome. Once clear of the station itself and the small coal yard, where a certain amount of coal was delivered by train each day for the area, he checked making sure that the Webley revolver was still tucked in his waistband. Having assured himself there was no problem there, it then occurred to him that he must somehow arm two of the grenades now reposing in his jacket pocket. Although under the circumstances Martin found this quite a simple task. On finding an opening at one side of the school gate, just wide enough for him to squeeze through, he carefully installed both primers, one in each grenade, made sure both pins were secure, then making his way to a nigh on six-foot fence which divided school from airfield, with agility he scaled the fence. Of course, on landing the other side, he realised there would be guards wandering around. Nevertheless much to Martins relief, and as though in answer to a prayer, quite suddenly an air-raid siren began whining out a warning, thereby coming to his rescue. Martin knew anyone on guard in an airfield, when a warning sounded, would most likely stay as close as possible to some sort of shelter, and that should give him long enough to dispose of at least two aircraft.

*

Before doing anything else, Dave and I quickly popped into Scotland Yard and low and behold there was the dear old 'super' waiting patiently to see us. He'd apparently received a report telling him that a railway porter had rung the Hornchurch police station, informing them that a suspicious character, that he the porter had last seen masquerading as an RAF corporal, had that night been accused of being seen leaving a house in Stanley Road Hornchurch, where a Mr: D. Ross had recently been found slain. It was a young London boy, aged about ten or eleven who was the accuser. As it happened, the boy in question did in fact live with his Mother opposite the house where Mr: Ross's body was found. 'Right' the 'super' had said, 'I want you to pull your bloody socks up and get down to Hornchurch bloody quick, now is that clear Inspector Selby'. Dave replied with a crisp 'Yes Sir' and within minutes we'd wheedled out DC Willis and were on our way.

We hopped a district line train straight through to Hornchurch. Once on the train, I pointed out to Dave and Tony, that it must have been that little cockney kid from Stanley Road, who's making these accusations. "Yeah, that makes sense," Tony remarked. "Well, makes no bleedin' difference who done the bleedin' accusing, it means if we're bloody quick enough, we'll be able to nobble our man that much sooner" Selby stated. "Yeah, well I wouldn't count yer chickens before they're 'atched me ol' mate" I warned him. "Never mind all that rubbish, if we do spot the bugger, we'll all tackle 'im this time," Selby told us. "Right," I said with a chuckle.

Once clear of train and platform Dave wandered off looking for our friendly ticket collector, whom he'd seen once before concerning this bloody elusive RAF corporal, and would yer believe, there his man stood collecting bleedin' train tickets. DC Willis glanced at me with raised eyebrows. "Now who'd 'ave believed that" I whispered to Willis. After they'd finished chatting, Dave sauntered over to Willis and myself with a big beaming smile across his face. "Yep, it's as yer reckoned Bill, that kid from Stanley Road spotted the bugger coming out that place they call a cinema round 'ere last night. That porter" Dave indicated with his thumb, then added "I've just been chatting to, says 'he found and spoke later with the kid', that's 'ow they know where your boy came from" Dave concluded. "I see, now it all makes sense" I knowingly acknowledged.

*

After scaling the school fence Martin crouched low, carefully surveyed his surrounding area, took the two primed grenades from his pocket. Moving quite slowly, advanced on a stationary spitfire, and from where he was then situated, he could clearly make out the shape of an aircraft hanger, which he knew would have at least two or three spitfires tucked away inside. Martin therefore decided to bide his time, he could now hear anti-aircraft guns in the distance, they were getting louder by the minute, then all of a sudden he heard the offbeat drone of German bombers above. He knew at once this was the moment to act.

Martin crouched low, darted forward into the shadows, he then found himself standing outside a hanger door, which he found amazingly easy to slide silently open. Martin took two grenades, tossed them one each side into said hanger, then tightly closed the door and quickly slipped back to the loan spitfire he'd originally started from. Here again, he found it quite easy opening the fuel cap of this aircraft, he thereupon used his handkerchief as a taper, made sure one end was securely installed into the fuel tank itself, with a few inches showing outside, he lit this dry portion with a match, then as two explosions erupted inside the hanger, he made a mad dash from this disaster scene he'd just created. Now also leaving a lone spitfire in flames, and nigh on close to exploding.

Once back at Hornchurch station Martin made a point of slipping through the barrier without being seen by any ticket collector, who'd been brave enough to stay on duty in this present air raid. Aboard the train, which was slowly moving due to the air raid, it was May & Baker that was uppermost in his mind yet again.

33:

A CHANGE OF LUCK

Once again our trip down to Hornchurch proved unsuccessful. Oh yes, we heard all about how some devious bugger had deliberately set fire to a lone spitfire, and then gone on to destroy an aircraft hanger with three spitfires, which were undergoing repairs, inside. Even so the Hornchurch police knew this was an act of sabotage, because although there'd been an air-raid in progress best part of the night, jerry had simply not dropped any bombs at all on, or even near Hornchurch aerodrome that night. Apparently it would appear all the damage sustained that night was in fact the work of a lone intruder, who'd obviously gained entry by way of the school fence. He then threw an explosive device inside a hanger. It is then believed he set fire to a loan spitfire before leaving the same way he'd come.

DI Selby along with DC Willis, made an appearance at Hornchurch airfield that morning, while I'd been designated the simple task of acting out my 'Sherlock Holmes' routine. All I had to do was ask questions around Hornchurch Station and take some bloody statements, is how Selby put it. However they returned empty-handed, and the only joy I obtained was when some little old feller told me 'a bloke of about six foot, nigh on shoved him off a bloody 66 bus, then rushed off without saying a bloody word' so like any good police sergeant would, I took this little old boys statement, in which he clearly stated 'when this bloke jumped off the bus, he straight away headed towards the school and airfield' so that was it. When Dave and Tony rejoined me, we pooled all our information together and come up with bugger all.

Anyway, back at Hornchurch police station, we were further informed that not only did this bugger re-arrange the bloody airfield somewhat, he'd also rushed over to Dagenham's May & Baker where he'd unloaded a couple more explosive devices for their approval. Now all in all it wasn't hard to see this bleeder was now taking the bloody piss out of us silly sods. Still, our trip hadn't been a complete waste of time. After we'd all had the usual bollocking from the local chief constable, Dave told me to nip round and get a statement from my little adopted cockney boy in Stanley Road. Alas, all I got was a neighbour telling me his mother had taken him to Southend for the day, which left me no other option than return to Dave and explain we were out of luck there. Dave groaned for a while, then decided we would spend that night there in Hornchurch and go back to London by car next morning.

*

Martin deposited two of his grenades just inside May & Baker's gate right alongside the building itself, which created a nice bright fire that he hoped would last the night through and guide many Luftwaffe pilots in and around the Dagenham Dock area. Martin accordingly decided he must for the time being stay here in Dagenham or near about. He could then perhaps use his last two grenades the following night. He therefore went in search of and quickly found a local pub that offered Bed and Breakfast. The place he'd chosen for this purpose was called 'The Merry

Fiddlers' and there it came to pass, while having a pint at the bar, a feller border happily informed him of a house in Nicholas Road Dagenham, where he, Martin, would no doubt be welcome to rent a room from a lady named Lily, at any time. His companion also mentioned that Lily had recently lost her husband at Dunkirk, and was only too happy to take in lodgers to make ends meet. Then more as an afterthought, his drinking partner mentioned she also had a strong hatred of politicians.

Martin thanked his fellow border, lit a fresh cigarette, bought another pint for them both, then indicated two chairs at a small table where they took refuge and discussed the art of playing that then common pub game 'darts'. They were still having a heated discussion on this subject when an air-raid warning sounded later that night. It was then they parted company. Martin went straight to his room, while his companion preferred the safety of an air-raid shelter. They therefore went in opposite directions.

*

We spent exactly two hours in a bloody air-raid shelter that night. Nevertheless, come morning, after a shave and brush up, followed by a two kipper breakfast, Dave and I were ready to meet the world. We walked down to see if we could ruin DC Willis's love life, as we did so, on approaching his little love nest, we noticed for some reason he'd parked our bloody car a good distance down the road, away from his lodgings. "Wonder why the bloody idiot left it back down there?" Selby asked. "I don't know, perhaps he enjoys a walk" I speculated. "Enjoys a bloody walk be buggered, the 'orny sod most probably got another bird living down there somewhere" Selby growled as we wandered along the road. "Yer know, yer could be right at that" I replied with a chuckle.

*

Martin now enjoying the sanctuary of his room, sat on the edge of his bed and pondered what he would gain if anything, by going to Nicholas Road, Dagenham and enquiring about staying at Lily's house for a week or so. On the one hand he thought, what a dirty dismal place Dagenham is, but then on the other hand he reasoned it could in fact be an ideal place to operate from. When one considered the opportunities that were on offer in this area, for instance, Briggs Motor Bodies, then there was Fords itself, and of course there was also Dagenham Docks, and umpteen other industrial factories he probably didn't even know about yet. So now having weighed up all the pros and cons, he decided it would be worth a try. Now with everything quiet in the vicinity, just a lone all clear disturbing the atmosphere, for those fortunate enough to still be alive and could appreciate it. Martin laid back and went into a deep peaceful sleep. Next morning he assumed it was the breakfast of egg and bacon that had put him in a positive frame of mind, for soon after he was dressed and ready to go. Once in Nicholas Road, Martin very quickly found the house he was looking for and as he'd been told, Lily the landlady was indeed eager to take in a lodger. So there and then a deal was struck for full board and lodging for one week, cash in hand.

Having paid a week in advance, Martin decided he would in fact stay that night, this he reasoned would allow him the next day, being a Sunday, to familiarise himself with his new surroundings. He therefore wished Lily a good night's sleep and retired to his own room.

*

All our speculating, concerning DC Willis having it off with another young lady, were dashed when he suddenly appeared walking towards us. However when we finally made contact, he informed us he'd come from Hornchurch police station via a complex system of alleyways that were prolific in Hornchurch. Nonetheless as DI Selby was about to ask why the car was parked so far away, Willis gestured for silence "Save it" he said, then excitedly burst out "I've just been told our man's been spotted in Nicholas Road, Dagenham". From the corner of my eye I saw Dave smile, and raise both hands in total disbelief. "Yeah, g'on pull the other one mate" he groaned. Nevertheless Willis persisted, raised his hand in front of Dave's face. "No listen to me, it's true, that bloke who said he saw this feller throw an explosive device alongside Heathway cinema, has just reported seein' 'im again in Dagenham this time, near where he himself lives" DC Willis insisted. I looked at Dave and could see he wasn't too sure. "Could be somethin' init Dave" I reasoned. After a moments silence, Dave seemingly half-convinced, grabbed Tony by the arm, pulled his face up close "Right, and who passed this loads of codswallop on to you then my old friend?" Dave demanded. Willis pulled away, gave Dave and me a hopeless look, then forcefully replied, "The bleedin' Hornchurch super of course that's who, and 'e also told me to come and fetch yer quick as possible, coz 'e wants to see yer". Dave just grunted, gave me a smile and said, "Right, don't let's 'ang about 'ere then". So it would seem from out of nowhere our luck had suddenly changed.

34:

AUGER'S MISTAKE

When Martin awoke that Sunday morning, he wasn't surprised to see the inclement weather still persisting, sky full of dark clouds with a continuous drizzle cascading from them. However whilst enjoying his first breakfast in his new lodgings in Nicholas Road, his new landlady, Lily, informed him rain had been forecast for the next two days and although it was still reasonably quiet outside at the moment, an air raid warning had in fact sounded about an hour ago, "now let's see" she said while glancing at a clock on the mantlepiece "oh yes, must have been around eight o'clock this morning they started" she further added. Martin gave her a puzzled look "And yet nothing's happened so far, that's strange, I wonder why?" he said as though speaking to himself.

It was sometime later while sitting in Lily's lounge, enjoying a cigarette and a cup of tea over-sweetened with saccharine, that Martin told her he'd been invited over to a friends' house for tea that afternoon. Lily wished him a pleasant afternoon before retiring from the room. After Lily's departure Martin relaxed awhile, he then decided that having given a reason for his absence from the house that evening, it would be preferable for him to leave immediately after lunch. He therefore moved to the kitchen where he knew Lily would then be preparing an early lunch. On entering the small kitchen, Martin studied Lily's figure from behind as she stood at the sink, very nice strong legs he thought, with a trim waist and a firm little

199

bottom. He was at that moment considering whether it would be wise of him to try his luck once again, but she suddenly turned to face him. "Oh I didn't know you were there dear, can I help you in any way?" she brightly enquired. "I'm so sorry, didn't mean to startle you, just wanted to tell you I'll probably be late tonight, will that be alright?" he softly enlightened her. "Yes, that will be fine dearie, I'll leave the key on the string, now don't you worry, you enjoy yourself" she advised.

*

When Dave and I arrived at Hornchurch police station it was a Superintendent Sinclaire we were urgently rushed in to see and yes, according to him, it would seem all of a sudden our luck had made a drastic turn for the better. DC Willis was right all along. The new 'super' (God bless him) didn't waste any time. On entering his office, he promptly advised us we'd be on our way to Dagenham within minutes, "However, before you leave I'll tell you exactly what's been happening". He then went on to explain in a calm clear voice, how the Dagenham police had come by some vital information which they then passed on to us.

Now once again back in Dagenham I entered the house with trepidation knowing full well my life could be in immediate danger, this on account DI Selby and me had seen our antagonist slip through the open front door of a bomb-damaged house, which stood alone in Nicholas Road some distance away from several recently bombed-out buildings. The reason we'd cottoned on to this bugger so quickly was due to a local good Samaritan, who'd reported having some sort of altercation with a bloke, he'd seen a week or so ago deposit an explosive device alongside the Heathway cinema. Of course the accused man vehemently denied being anywhere near Heathway that time or at any other time, for that matter.

Coincidently it so happened that while this good Samaritan was actually standing explaining to us exactly what had transpired between them, the very man he was then accusing, strolled smartly passed us without showing any sign of recognition whatsoever, and although our informer was about to say something to this man, Selby immediately signalled him into silence, and strange though it may seem, it was at that moment I finally got a clear unrestricted view of this miserable bloody creatures face who I'd danced the highland fling with, in that bloody hut on Biggin Hill airfield sometime back.

Anyway, Dave quickly instructed our informer to stay in the area "There, pop over to that tea shop" Dave pointed "wait for us there, we'll not be long," he promised as we edged away and started following our bloody elusive adversary. "We won't grab the bugger just yet, let's wait, see where he's goin', might be a gang of the sods hoard up somewhere" Dave rattled off. "I bloody 'ope not" I replied as we tagged along behind this tall sod, a man I'd been waiting to have another sparring session with since he'd presented me with that bleeding tin hat in the face last time we'd met.

*

Depositing his last two grenades at Every Ready's battery plant had caused Martin no problem at all, simply because that Sunday afternoon being damp, cloudy and miserable, had not surprisingly robbed the local inhabitants of any desire to stray far from home. So with no one about to observe his actions, Martin had primed his last two grenades, then quickly threw them onto the roof of this small battery factory and thereafter began a tedious journey back to Nicholas Road. It was however at that moment, he'd heard three or four bombs explode a short distance away. The sound, it would seem, came directly from the direction, where he was now heading.

As Martin traversed Wood Lane, he became aware that a mixture of vehicles, which consisted of fire engines, ambulances and police cars were gathering hereabouts. Nevertheless Martin continued on his way, but on turning from Wood Lane into Valence Wood Road, he suddenly noticed three men standing to one side in deep conversation, near a group of people that were milling around, all seemingly intent on helping others exit from what appeared to be a bombed building, at one end of the road. He immediately recognised two of the three men. One he'd had a dispute with some time earlier, yet somehow it was the other shorter blonde-haired man he would if possible like to avoid, for he remembered when they'd had their last encounter at Biggin Hill, he had disabled this blonde feller with the help of a tin hat, and he instinctively knew that blondie would be looking for revenge.

There was no doubt in Martins mind that his blonde adversary and a taller man whom he'd never seen before were in fact police officers. As it was, he'd actually turned into Valence Wood Road, and started for Nicholas Road when he saw at once it was Nicholas Road itself that had indeed received the bomb, and to his horror his lodgings had been completely demolished. Martin therefore made a point of ignoring these three men who had seemingly lost all interest in him. One of them in fact, it would appear, began directing one of the others to a small tea room which stood at the end of Wood Lane. Nevertheless be that as it may, at this point Martin knew he would now be under continuous observation, so bearing this in mind, he quickly decided to forego making enquiries regarding Lily's whereabouts. Instead he reasoned, it was imperative for him to execute every trick he knew, in order to avoid capture. He then accordingly leapt over the front gate of a bomb-damaged house which stood at the end of Nicholas Road. He went straight on through a wide-open front door that he took the trouble to close behind him.

*

DI Selby pulled up short. "Look Bill, d'yer see that?" he asked with surprise. "Course I bloody saw it, the bleeders dodged into that bloody 'ouse" I told him. Dave gave me a nonplussed glance. "Well, what yer got in mind then?" I queried. "Go straight in after the sod I suppose, what d'yer reckon?" he came back with. "No, 'ang about, let me foller 'im in, you nip round the back Dave, just in case" I almost implored him. I saw him hesitate, so I quickly added, "after all it was me he clobbered with that bloody tin 'elmet". At this point Dave relented "Ok mate, it's your call" he granted. Although not completely at ease with the situation, it was nevertheless at that moment when I barged through that front door, in Nicholas Road, Dagenham, thereby putting my life at risk on entering the aforesaid bomb-damaged house, is when a wave of trepidation ran through me.

On hearing a door bang upstairs, I quite naturally headed for the stairs. Once at the top I flung open the first room door I came to, which to my cost turned out to be a careless mistake. As I then stood framed in an open doorway, a broom handle was thrust into my solar plexus. I went to my knees gasping for air whilst telling myself this must be your bloody lot Auger.

35:

HE JUST FADED AWAY

Martin stood in an upstairs room deliberating what he should do next. As he did so the front door of the house crashed open. He knew at once someone had followed him in, but how many he wondered? It was then Martin remembered the gun still snugly tucked away in his waistband. However, he decided not to rely solely on the gun, reasoning that with the limited amount of ammunition he possessed, it would perhaps be prudent of him to use this weapon only as a last resort, so with this thought in mind, his eyes began searching the room for an alternative means of defence. Although at this moment it had occurred to him that if more than one man had come through that front door, he might very well have need of the fire-arm. Meanwhile, he selected for his purpose, a broom which stood just behind the room door, which at that moment was flung open. Martin did not hesitate, he jabbed the handle of said broom into the man's midriff as he entered.

*

I began to feel slightly faint, but from a distance I heard a voice say, "Not you again!" this was followed by a low chuckle. I made a gigantic effort to suck in as much oxygen as I possibly could, in order to revitalise my now tired limbs. Then another voice growled "Grab the bastard Tony" and to my relief my two partners had rejoined me.

Alas, sad to say that's when our luck swung the other way. Now once again back on my feet it was Tony's turn to take the brunt of this mans' rage. As Tony rushed forward to grab our man, he received a vicious straight left hand jab on his jaw which instantly sat poor old Tony on his backside. Of course by the time he and I had recovered our senses, this friendly bastard, we'd spent what seemed like a lifetime chasing halfway across England looking for, now stood facing us holding a bloody gun, which is something us silly sods hadn't even thought of carrying. So here we all were, Tony nursing a seemingly broken jaw, me still struggling to breathe and Selby no doubt thoroughly frustrated, and the bugger us three silly sods were supposed to be arresting, standing there with a bleeding big grin on his face, while trying to decide which one of us he should shoot first. Anyway what followed, I still regard as plain trickery. "You and you over there" he indicated Selby and I should join Tony who was now seated on a large window sill, so we joined Tony. The gun waved at us again, the man holding it said with conviction "Now boys, you stay here, I'm off to Dover and back to the Fatherland" and with that, he stepped through the bloody door, which he closed and carefully locked behind him. I at once tried opening a window with no bloody luck, however on squinting between the strips of brown sticky paper that criss-crossed each pane of glass, in order to prevent any glass flying about from the blast of a bomb, I immediately noticed on looking down it was bloody obvious we were up way too high for any heroics, like throwing ourselves out of a top floor window. Tony stood, and while caressing his jaw, mumbled, "'Ow the bloody 'ell we gonna get out then?" For a reply, I gave him a knowing smile, gently guided him to one side, snatched up this unfriendly bloody broom and began prodding the ceiling with the handle. In minutes we were through the ceiling and down through the loft hatch. Once again back on the street, where we all made stringent enquiries of various police officers as to whether they'd seen our gun-toting playmate legging it off somewhere, and as per normal, apparently no-one saw a bloody thing. So our next move was a trip to Dover. Willis somehow managed to snatch a car and off we went.

At Dover some bright spark of a Harbour Master, smugly informed us no one would dare go across to France from Dover now "France is occupied by the bleeding Germans now" he joyously informed us "no mate, he probably had a U-boat pick him up somewhere along the coast" this smart arse added. That's when DI Selby looked at me, threw both his arms in the air and screamed "The buggers done it again, he's just faded away"

Next day in spite of being kept awake half the bloody night by bloody air raids, we drove back to Hornchurch in order to re-arrange our accommodation back to how we first found it, and of course to report our miserable failure in losing our man. I also thought it a good idea to say goodbye to my little cockney friend from Stanley Road. So after wishing our respective landladies good luck, I then left Dave and Tony waiting for me at the Hornchurch police station canteen.

I found my little snotty nose bundle of joy swinging on his front gate. "'Ellow mister wot yer doin' round 'ere again?" he asked without me having to decode one word. "Would yer believe, I've come lookin' for you" I told him, and for the first time I really saw this poor little sod for what he was and what he'd gone through so far, and furthermore just what the poor little bugger would have to look forward to at the end of this bloody war. I thereupon hooked out two half-crown pieces, placed them in his small hand. "Blimey, thanks mister, 'ere, yer can come lookin' for me any day yer like, if yer gonna throw money about like this" he offered. I smiled "'Ere what's yer name, anyway?" I asked. "No" he quickly replied. "No!, what d'yer mean no?" I responded in puzzlement. "Well, it ain't 'anyway'" he brightly answered. "Oh bloody funny," I said. He then added grimly "see my mum says I look like that Errol Flynn actor, so she calls me Albert" he chuckled. I was amazed "Albert! That doesn't sound nothing like Errol Flynn" I shot back. "'Ere, yer ain't arf bleedin' brainy aintcher," he cleverly replied. I made to cuff him around the ear. "Yer cheeky little bugger" I warned him. But this streetwise little toe rag had dodged smartly out of reach saying "If my dad was 'ere he'd 'ave yer for that" he threatened with a sad look then coming into his eyes. Once again I started feeling sorry for this poor scruffy bugger. "Where is yer Dad?" I jokingly enquired. A half smile cut across this kid's little face "Oh 'im, won't be seein' 'im no more, my mum says silly bleeder stopped one at Dunkirk didn't 'e," the little feller said abruptly with a shrug of his small shoulders, and straight away his answer made me wish I'd never asked.

I then regarded this sad little creature with a degree of pity, ruffled the kids' hair, dug deeper in my pocket for another half-crown coin, gave it to him. I couldn't say anything; the lump in my throat wouldn't let me. I turned away thinking 'fuckin' war, why do we allow this sort of thing to happen'.

———

THE BLITZ

London dear London,
just what have they done?
With bombs, bright searchlights,
And those big, booming guns.

People in shelters shivering in fright,
Yet praying for peace,
night after night,
Planes showering death down at a terrible rate,
No wonder old London was so full of hate.

At home they're nice fellows,
of this there's no doubt,
But not over here, where they're bombing us out.
High in the heavens showing no pity,
They just seemed intent on ruining our city.

With bombs raining down,
blowing old London to bits,
This was the time
which is known as the blitz.

Mothers with babies, oh so much crying,
While old people are asking,
"Is our London dying?"

Now it's all over, the years have rolled on,
Most Londoners wonder,
Where their dear London's gone

So if you were there,
now one of the few,
You'll think of old London,
Just what did they do?

Of course they've rebuilt it,
so bright and so new,
Yet old folks still remember,
The London they knew.

Taken from *Where the Poppies Grow an anthology of poems about two World Wars* by Ronand Cove.

Acknowledgements

Once again I owe a debt of gratitude to my very patient wife, and a daughter that is second to none, for all the help I've received from them in bringing this book to fruition. They are both beyond any praise I could bestow upon them.

I would also like to offer my thanks to a helpful understanding lady named Pat, for all the running around she's done on my behalf.

Last but not least, my thanks to John for always being there when needed.

And to conclude I would like to offer my sincere thanks to my friendly neighbours and the readers who have kindly supported me since I began writing.

Other Books by Ronald Cove

*Available worldwide from Amazon
and all good bookstores*

---

www.mtp.agency

www.facebook.com/mtp.agency

@mtp_agency

www.ingramcontent.com/pod-product-compliance
Lightning Source LLC
LaVergne TN
LVHW041630060526
838200LV00040B/1521